GUITAR
TRAINING EXERCISES

OVER 150 PROVEN WARM-UPS & WORKOUTS

BY JOE CHARUPAKORN

ISBN 978-1-5400-6313-7

HAL•LEONARD®

Visit Hal Leonard Online at
www.halleonard.com

Contact us:
Hal Leonard
7777 West Bluemound Road
Milwaukee, WI 53213
Email: info@halleonard.com

In Europe, contact:
Hal Leonard Europe Limited
42 Wigmore Street
Marylebone, London, W1U 2RN
Email: info@halleonardeurope.com

In Australia, contact:
Hal Leonard Australia Pty. Ltd.
4 Lentara Court
Cheltenham, Victoria, 3192 Australia
Email: info@halleonard.com.au

PREFACE

Technical studies are an important part of every musician's development. This book presents a wide variety of exercises for guitar—with several fingering options for each—designed to enhance not only your technical ability, but also your fretboard visualization skills.

In addition to the exercises, there are three pieces from the classical violin repertoire in the last section of this book that will give you a truly challenging technical workout: The Allegro Assai from J.S. Bach's Sonata #5 for solo violin, *Moto Perpetuo* by Paganini, and Wohlfahrt's Study #3.

—Joe Charupakorn

ABOUT THE AUTHOR

New York City native Joe Charupakorn is a guitarist, editor, and best-selling author. He has written numerous instructional books for Hal Leonard. His books are available worldwide and have been translated into many languages. Visit him on the web at *joecharupakorn.com*.

CONTENTS

INTRODUCTION

The best way to use this book is to create a practice strategy. This means choosing a few exercises (you don't have to learn *every* exercise in the book) and working on them daily until you feel you have technically mastered them.

A good practice routine consists of starting out with some of the warm-up exercises to get the blood flowing, then taking a scale pattern and playing through each fingering of the pattern. Do this slowly and try to visualize the shapes of the scales as you play the pattern. Work on the arpeggio patterns in a similar fashion.

Learn each exercise with all the fingerings given slowly and carefully, never sacrificing clarity and accuracy for speed. The goal is to develop an instinctive command of the fretboard.

A metronome is a good tool to help chart your progress—be sure to get one if you don't already have one. Use it to keep track of tempo markings daily to monitor your progress. See what tempos you are comfortable with and what your upper limits are.

HOW TO USE THIS BOOK

This book is arranged as follows: first a presentation of the scales and arpeggios in several positions then exercises based on these positions. Learn each position of the scales and arpeggios thoroughly before attempting the exercises. Try learning one scale and one arpeggio exercise per week and you will notice a significant improvement in your technical ability.

At the end of the book are some etudes from the masters that will prove to be an extreme technical challenge. Don't be intimidated by these pieces; with consistent practice you will be able to play them. Start slowly, building up speed daily and using your metronome as a guide.

WARM-UP EXERCISES
The warm-up exercises consist of the 24 finger patterns possible using a one-finger-per-fret finger pattern scheme in first position. Keep your left-hand fingers as close to the fretboard as possible to economize the finger movements (especially the pinky and ring finger).

SCALES
The exercises in this book are based on the three most common scales: the major scale, the ascending or jazz melodic minor scale, and the harmonic minor scale. Four positions are given for each.

SCALE SEQUENCES
The scale sequences are based on the three scales and the four positions given, but may veer off when a more practical fingering for the situation is available. The fingerings presented are only a guide; in real life situations, some musical phrases may work better with slight modifications or position shifts. Study each of the patterns to see how they relate to each other.

ARPEGGIOS
All arpeggios—from triads to seventh chords—are presented in four different positions, just like the scales. These are the most common patterns and should be memorized.

ARPEGGIO SEQUENCES

These sequences are based on the four arpeggio patterns presented in the arpeggios section.

DIATONIC ARPEGGIO SEQUENCES

Diatonic arpeggio sequences are presented in the key of C major. After learning them in C major, try these patterns using the C jazz melodic minor and C harmonic minor scales as a resource. Practice them in other keys as well.

LINEAR DIATONIC ARPEGGIOS

Linear arpeggios move horizontally across the fretboard, rather than the position-based vertical fingerings presented earlier, and are shown here in the key of C major (again, after learning them in C, try using the C jazz melodic minor and C harmonic minor). Learning these linear arpeggios will help solidify your knowledge of the fretboard and improve your technique.

PIECES

As a conclusion to the book, three challenging pieces from the violin repertoire are presented. The Allegro Assai from J.S. Bach's Sonata #5 for solo violin, Paganini's *Moto Perpetuo,* and Wohlfahrt's Study #3.

Warm-up Exercises

#1

#2

Warm-up Exercises

#3

#4

Warm-up Exercises

#5

#6

Warm-up Exercises

#7

#8

Warm-up Exercises

#9

#10

Warm-up Exercises

#11

#12

Warm-up Exercises

#13

#14

Warm-up Exercises

#15

#16

Warm-up Exercises

#17

#18

Warm-up Exercises

#19

#20

Warm-up Exercises

#21

#22

Warm-up Exercises

#23

#24

Exercise #1: C Major Scale

Fingering #1

Fingering #2

Fingering #3

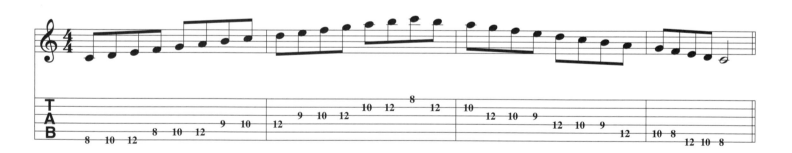

Fingering #4

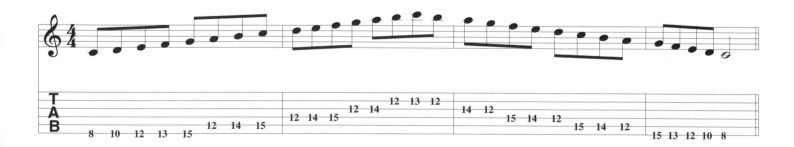

Exercise #2: C Jazz Melodic Minor Scale

Fingering #1

Fingering #2

Fingering #3

Fingering #4

Exercise #3: C Harmonic Minor Scale

Fingering #1

Fingering #2

Fingering #3

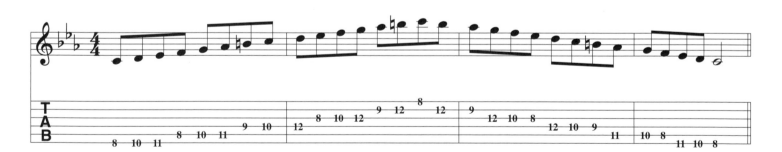

Fingering #4

Exercise #4: C Chromatic Scale

Exercise #5: Scale Sequence in C Major

Fingering #1

Fingering #2

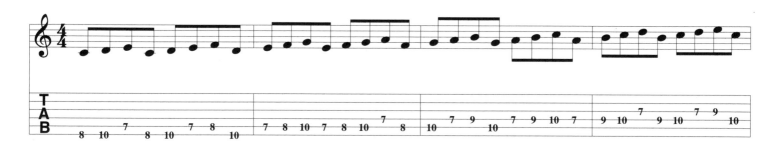

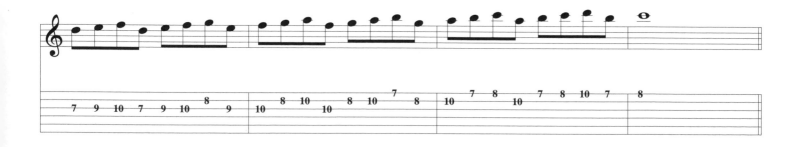

Exercise #5: Scale Sequence in C Major

Fingering #3

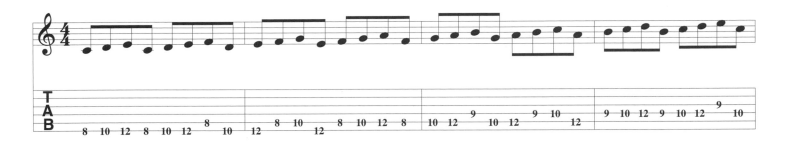

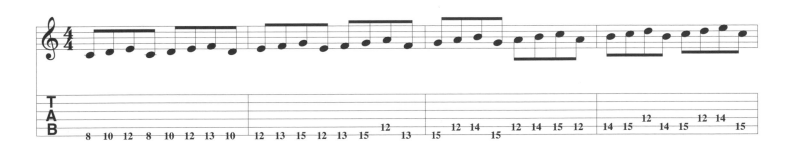

Fingering #4

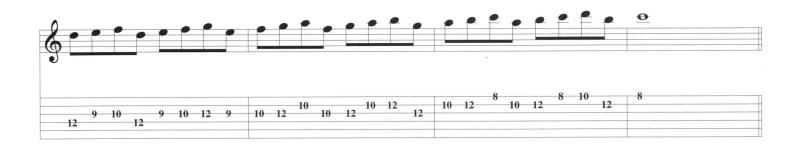

Exercise #6: Scale Sequence in C Jazz Melodic Minor

Fingering #1

Fingering #2

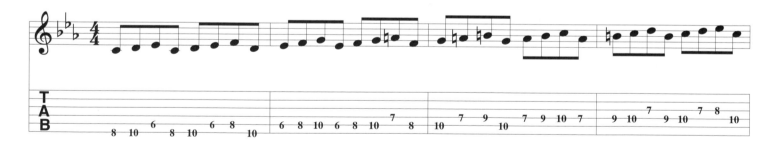

Exercise #6: Scale Sequence in C Jazz Melodic Minor

Fingering #3

Fingering #4

Exercise #7: Scale Sequence in C Harmonic Minor

Fingering #1

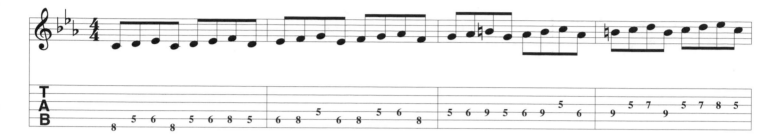

Fingering #2

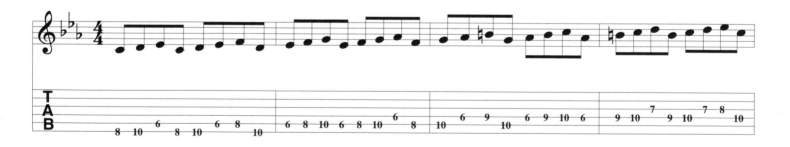

Exercise #7: Scale Sequence in C Harmonic Minor

Fingering #3

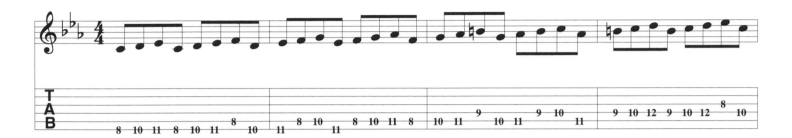

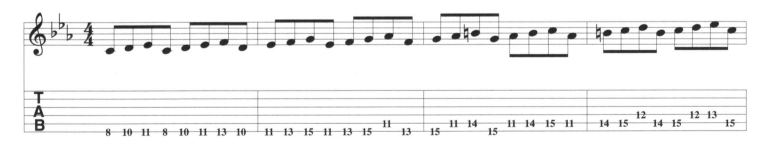

Fingering #4

Exercise #8: Scale Sequence in C Major

Fingering #1

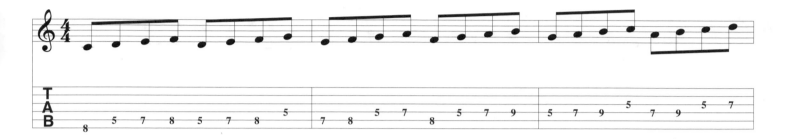

Fingering #2

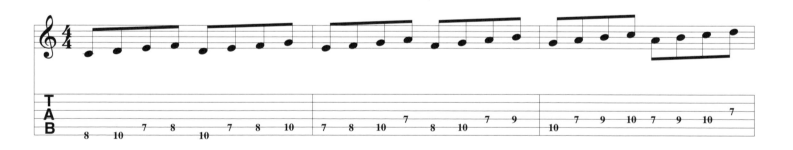

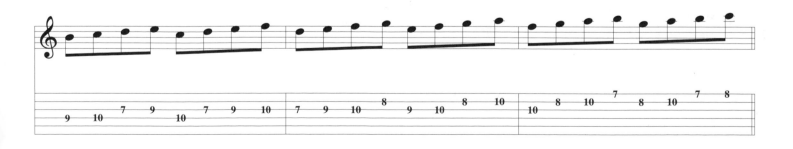

Exercise #8: Scale Sequence in C Major

Fingering #3

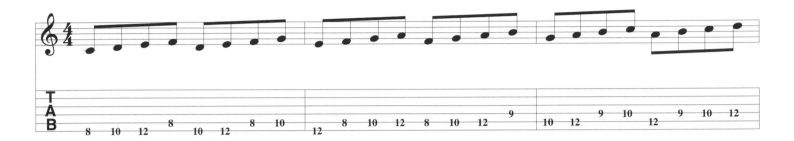

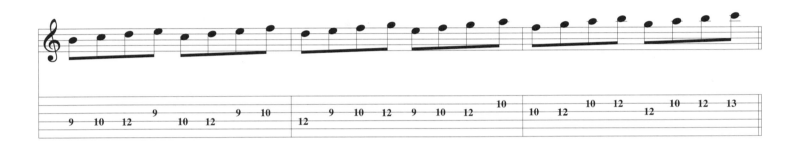

Fingering #4

Exercise #9: Scale Sequence in C Jazz Melodic Minor

Fingering #1

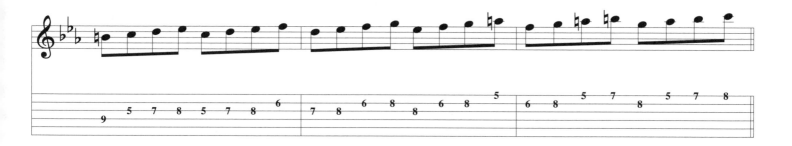

Fingering #2

Exercise #9: Scale Sequence in C Jazz Melodic Minor

Fingering #3

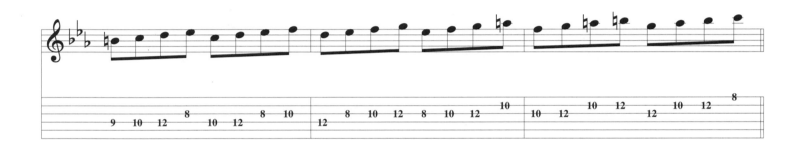

Fingering #4

Exercise #10: Scale Sequence in C Harmonic Minor

Fingering #1

Fingering #2

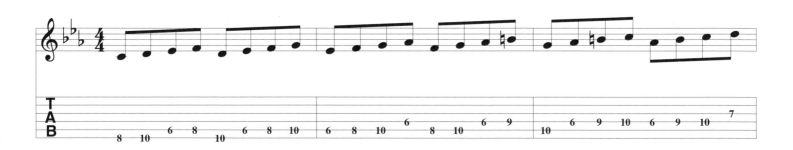

Exercise #10: Scale Sequence in C Harmonic Minor

Fingering #3

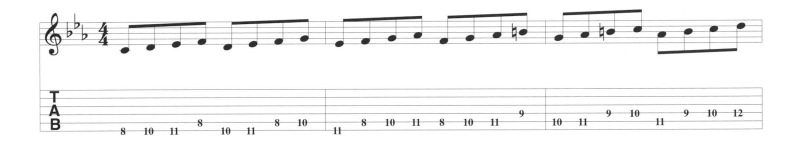

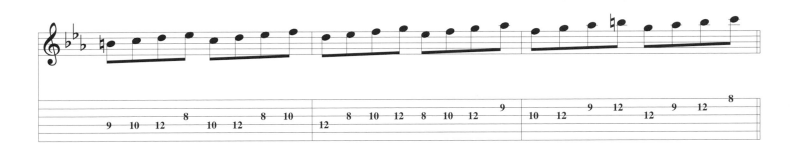

Fingering #4

Exercise #11: Scale Sequence in C Major

Fingering #1

Fingering #2

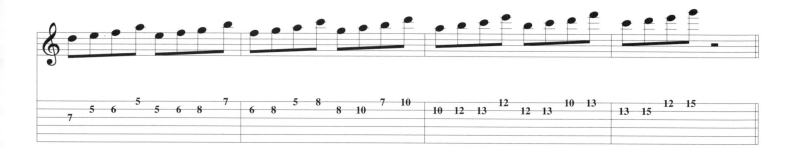

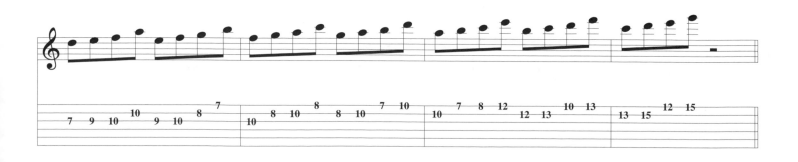

Exercise #11: Scale Sequence in C Major

Fingering #3

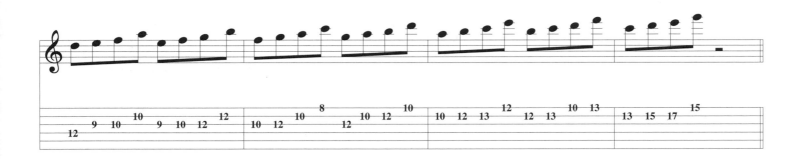

Fingering #4

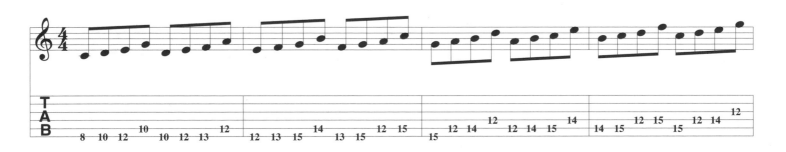

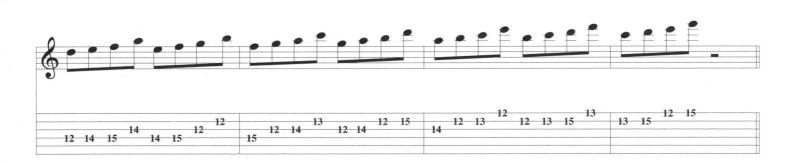

Exercise #12: Scale Sequence in C Jazz Melodic Minor

Fingering #1

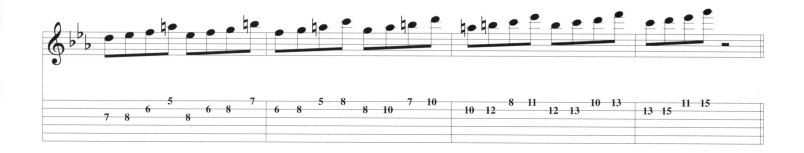

Fingering #2

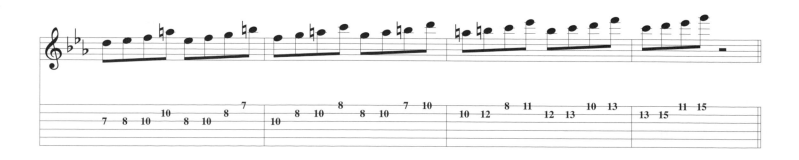

Exercise #12: Scale Sequence in C Jazz Melodic Minor

Fingering #3

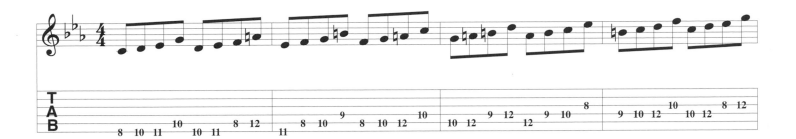

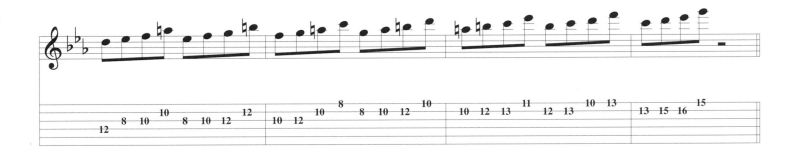

Fingering #4

Exercise #13: Scale Sequence in C Harmonic Minor

Fingering #1

Fingering #2

Exercise #13: Scale Sequence in C Harmonic Minor

Fingering #3

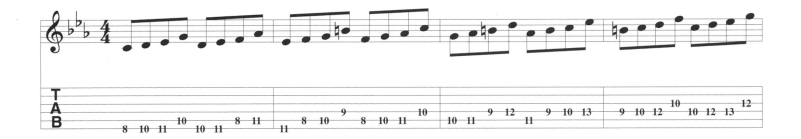

Fingering #4

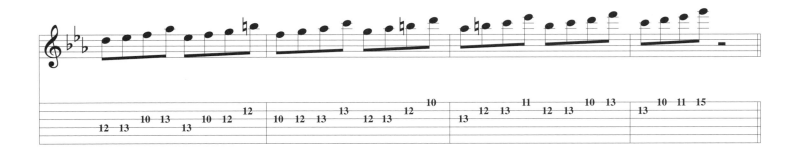

Exercise #14: Scale Sequence in C Major

Fingering #1

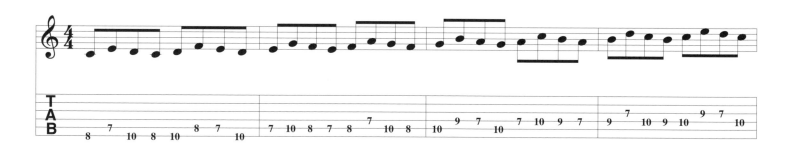

Fingering #2

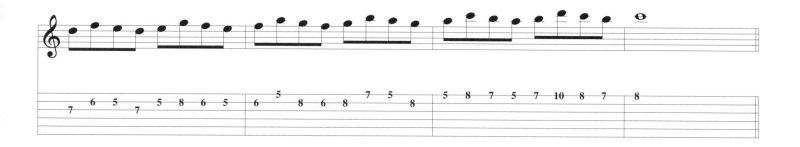

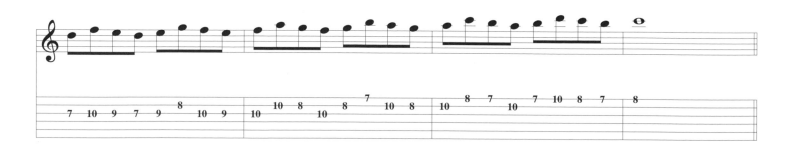

Exercise #14: Scale Sequence in C Major

Fingering #3

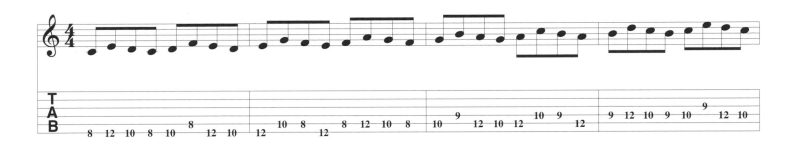

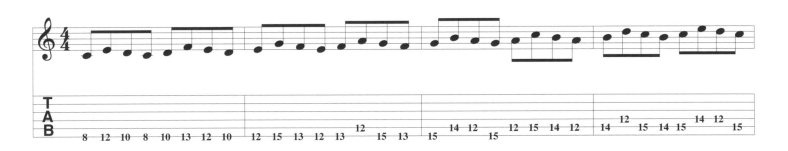

Fingering #4

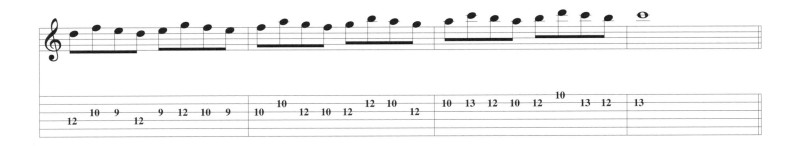

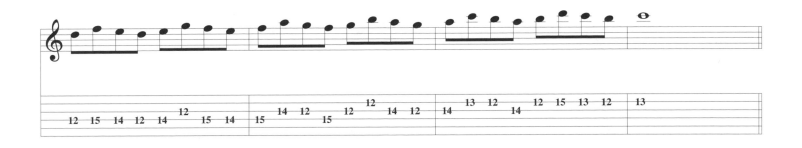

Exercise #15: Scale Sequence in C Jazz Melodic Minor

Fingering #1

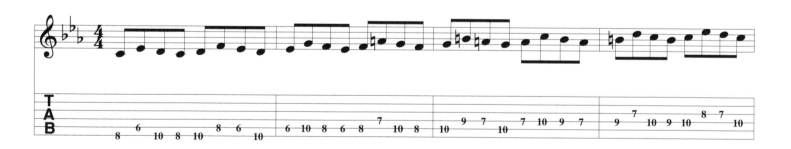

Fingering #2

Exercise #15: Scale Sequence in C Jazz Melodic Minor

Fingering #3

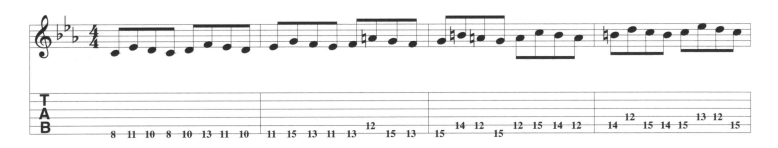

Fingering #4

Exercise #16: Scale Sequence in C Harmonic Minor

Fingering #1

Fingering #2

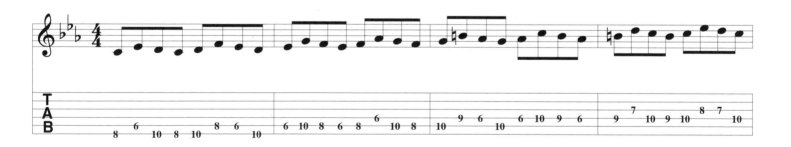

Exercise #16: Scale Sequence in C Harmonic Minor

Fingering #3

Fingering #4

Exercise #17: Scale Sequence in C Major

Fingering #1

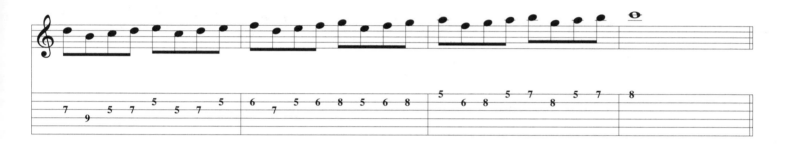

Fingering #2

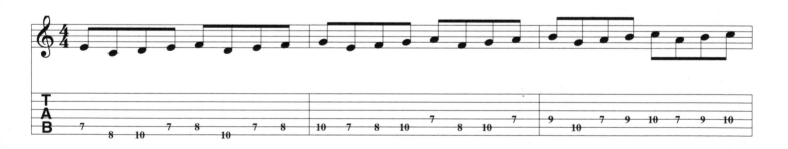

Exercise #17: Scale Sequence in C Major

Fingering #3

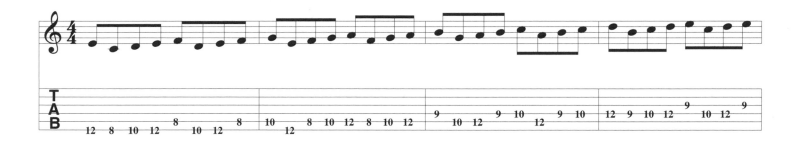

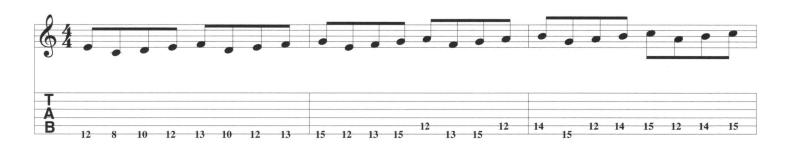

Fingering #4

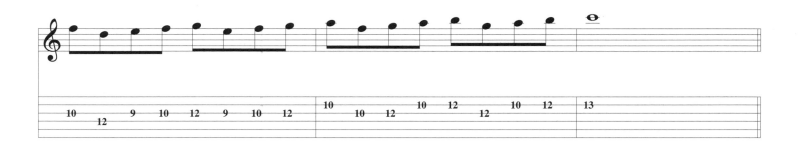

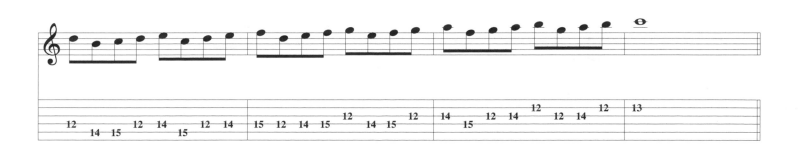

Exercise #18: Scale Sequence in C Jazz Melodic Minor

Fingering #1

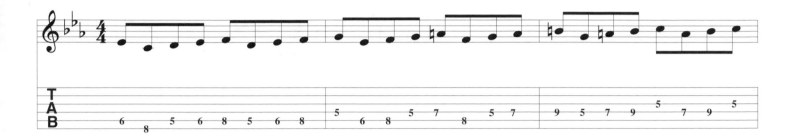

Fingering #2

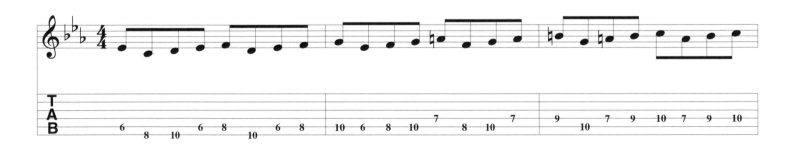

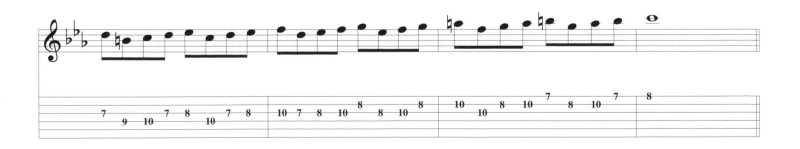

Exercise #18: Scale Sequence in C Jazz Melodic Minor

Fingering #3

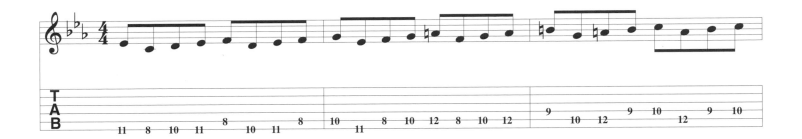

Fingering #4

Exercise #19: Scale Sequence in C Harmonic Minor

Fingering #1

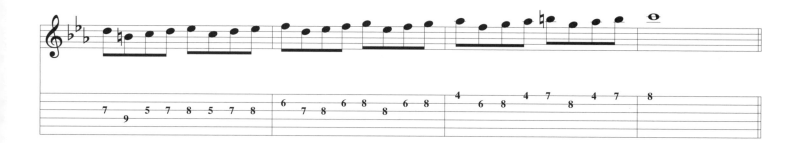

Fingering #2

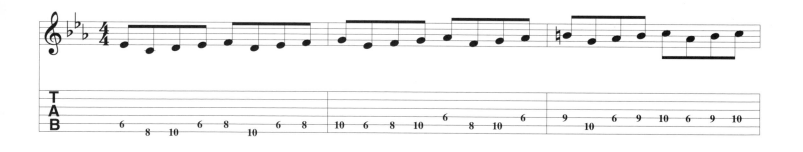

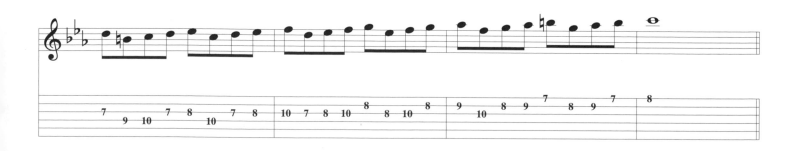

Exercise #19: Scale Sequence in C Harmonic Minor

Fingering #3

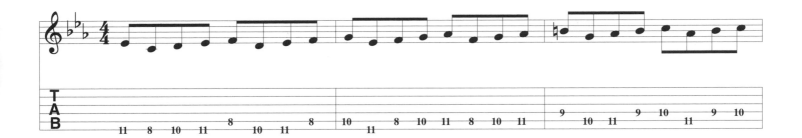

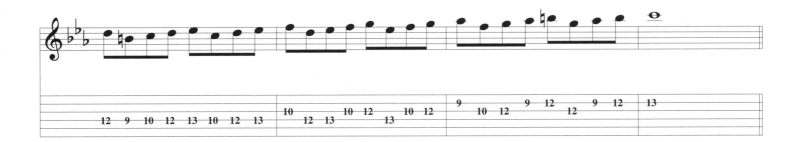

Fingering #4

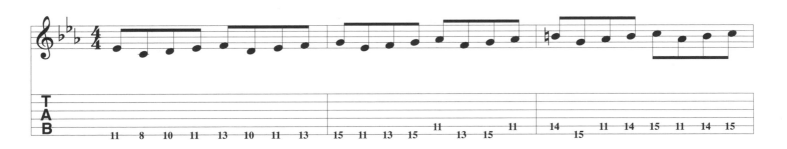

Exercise #20: Scale Sequence in C Major

Fingering #1

Fingering #2

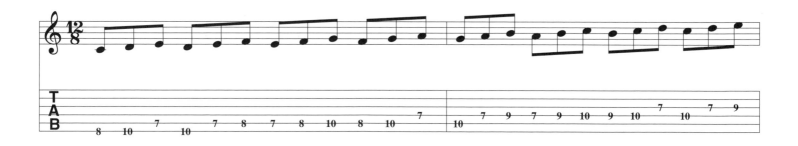

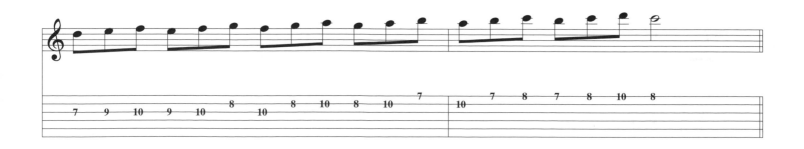

Exercise #20: Scale Sequence in C Major

Fingering #3

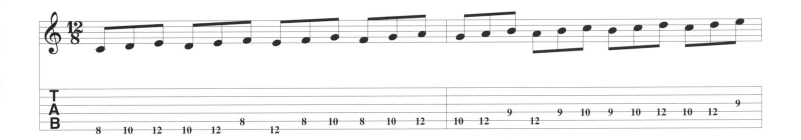

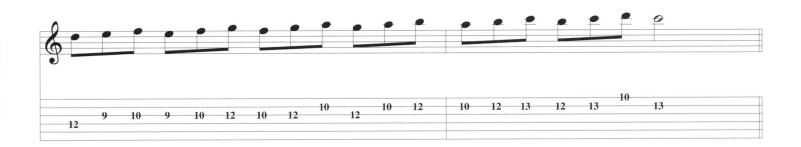

Fingering #4

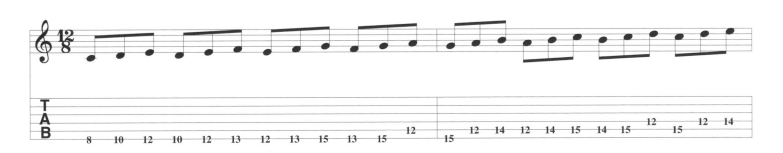

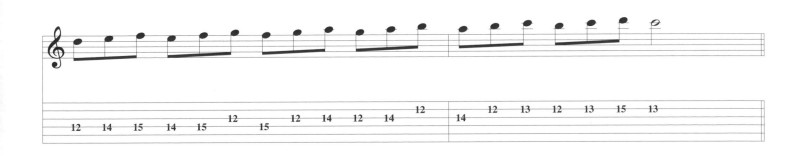

Exercise #21: Scale Sequence in C Jazz Melodic Minor

Fingering #1

Fingering #2

Exercise #21: Scale Sequence in C Jazz Melodic Minor

Fingering #3

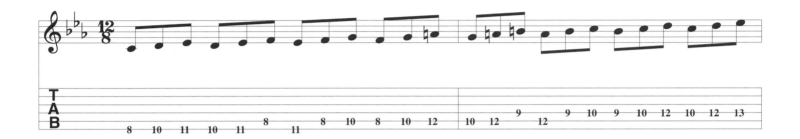

Fingering #4

Exercise #22: Scale Sequence in C Harmonic Minor

Fingering #1

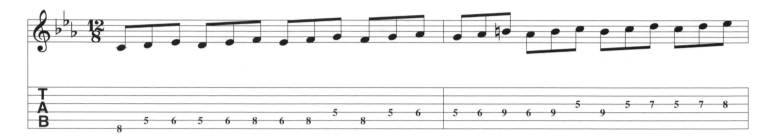

Fingering #2

Exercise #22: Scale Sequence in C Harmonic Minor

Fingering #3

Fingering #4

Exercise #23: Scale Sequence in C Major

Fingering #1

Fingering #2

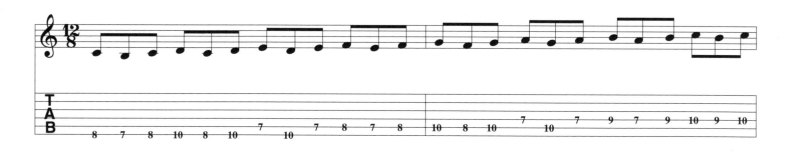

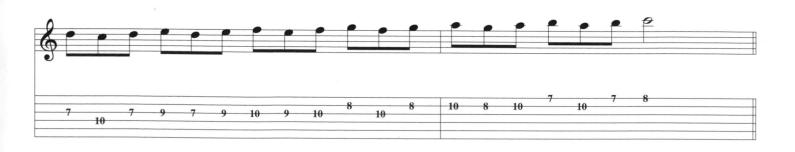

Exercise #23: Scale Sequence in C Major

Fingering #3

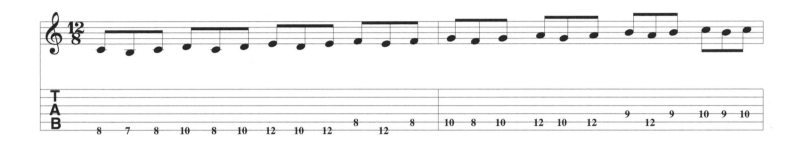

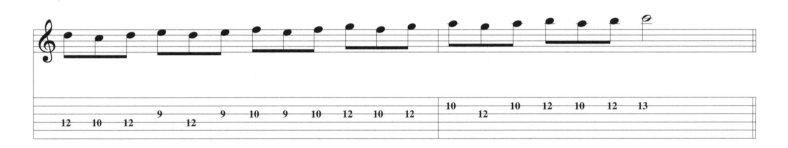

Fingering #4

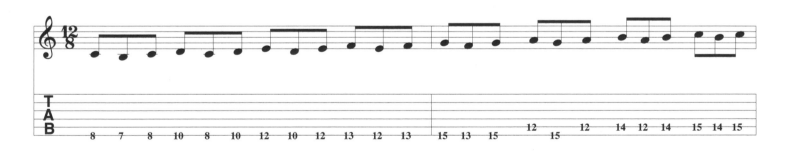

Exercise #24: Scale Sequence in C Jazz Melodic Minor

Fingering #1

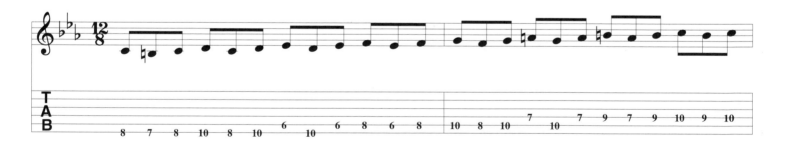

Fingering #2

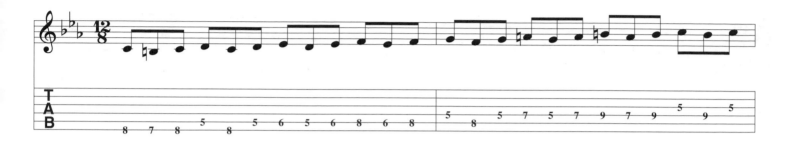

Exercise #24: Scale Sequence in C Jazz Melodic Minor

Fingering #3

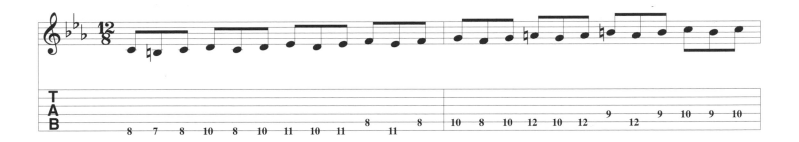

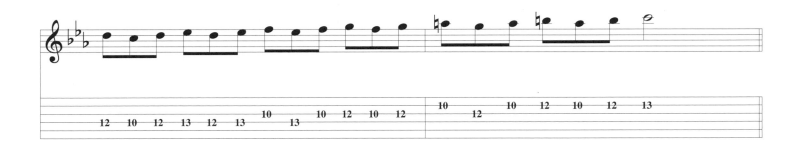

Fingering #4

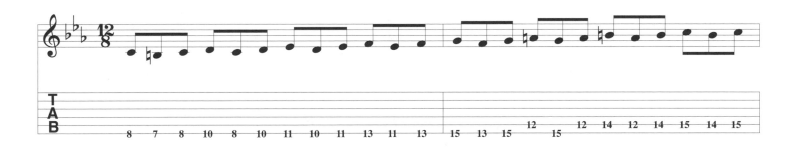

Exercise #25: Scale Sequence in C Harmonic Minor

Fingering #1

Fingering #2

Exercise #25: Scale Sequence in C Harmonic Minor

Fingering #3

Fingering #4

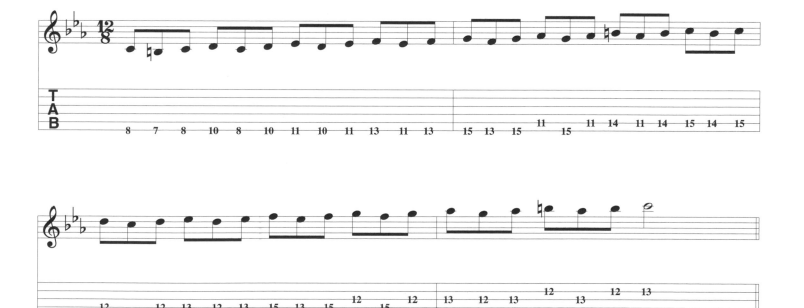

Exercise #26: Scale Sequence in C Major

Fingering #1

Fingering #2

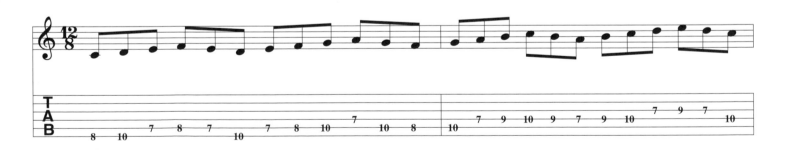

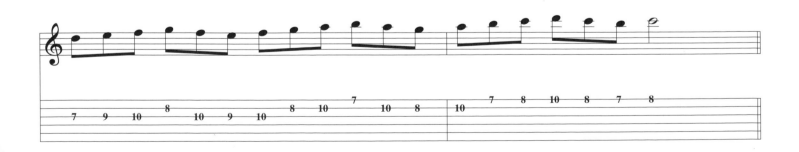

Exercise #26: Scale Sequence in C Major

Fingering #3

Fingering #4

Exercise #27: Scale Sequence in C Jazz Melodic Minor

Fingering #1

Fingering #2

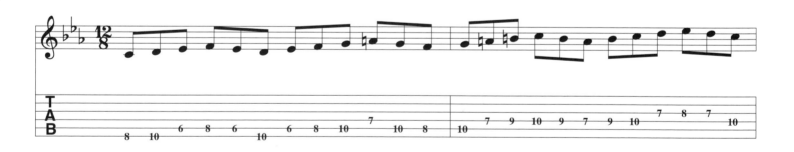

Exercise #27: Scale Sequence in C Jazz Melodic Minor

Fingering #3

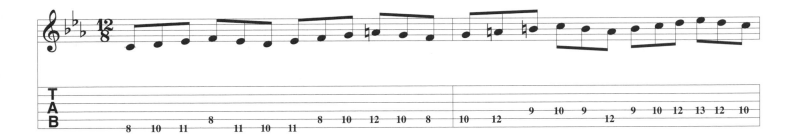

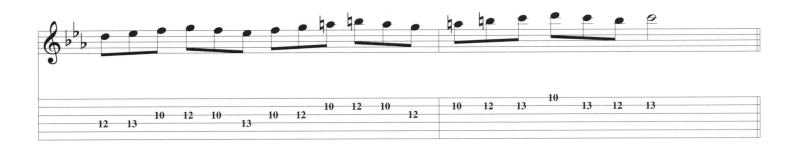

Fingering #4

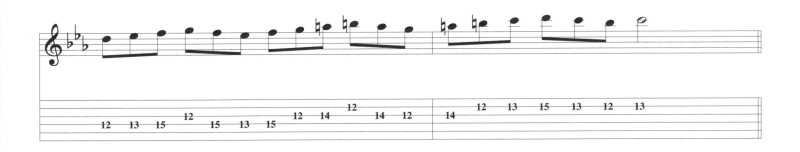

Exercise #28: Scale Sequence in C Harmonic Minor

Fingering #1

Fingering #2

Exercise #28: Scale Sequence in C Harmonic Minor

Fingering #3

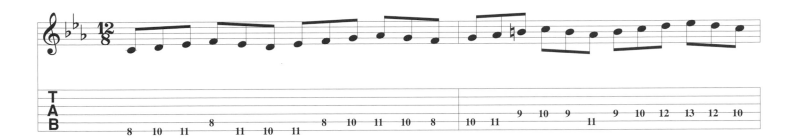

Fingering #4

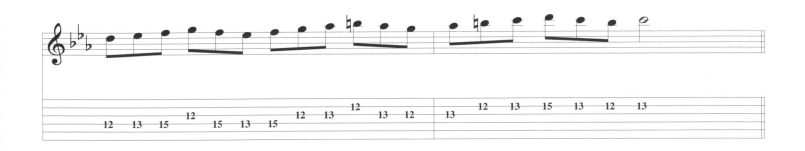

Exercise #29: Ascending 3rds in C Major

Fingering #1

Fingering #2

Fingering #3

Fingering #4

Exercise #30: Ascending 3rds in C Jazz Melodic Minor

Fingering #1

Fingering #2

Fingering #3

Fingering #4

Exercise #31: Ascending 3rds in C Harmonic Minor

Fingering #1

Fingering #2

Fingering #3

Fingering #4

Exercise #32: Descending 3rds in C Major

Fingering #1

Fingering #2

Fingering #3

Fingering #4

Exercise #33: Descending 3rds in C Jazz Melodic Minor

Fingering #1

Fingering #2

Fingering #3

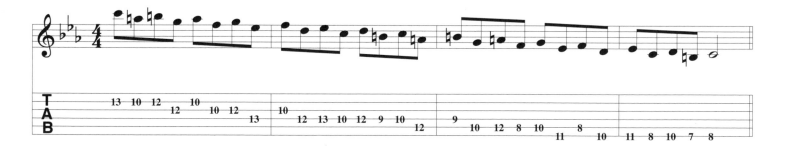

Fingering #4

Exercise #34: Descending 3rds in C Harmonic Minor

Fingering #1

Fingering #2

Fingering #3

Fingering #4

Exercise #35: Descending 3rds in C Major

Fingering #1

Fingering #2

Fingering #3

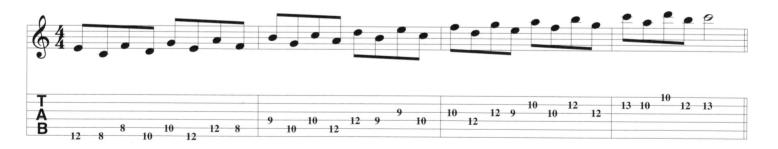

Fingering #4

Exercise #36: Descending 3rds in C Jazz Melodic Minor

Fingering #1

Fingering #2

Fingering #3

Fingering #4

Exercise #37: Descending 3rds in C Harmonic Minor

Fingering #1

Fingering #2

Fingering #3

Fingering #4

Exercise #38: Ascending 3rds in C Major

Fingering #1

Fingering #2

Fingering #3

Fingering #4

Exercise #39: Ascending 3rds in C Jazz Melodic Minor

Fingering #1

Fingering #2

Fingering #3

Fingering #4

Exercise #40: Ascending 3rds in C Harmonic Minor

Fingering #1

Fingering #2

Fingering #3

Fingering #4

Exercise #41: Ascending 4ths in C Major

Fingering #1

Fingering #2

Fingering #3

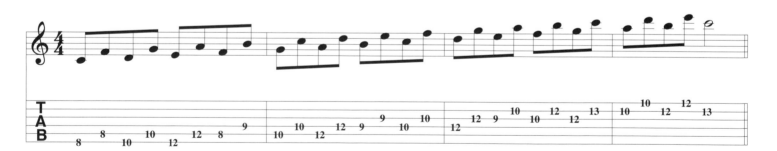

Fingering #4

Exercise #42: Ascending 4ths in C Jazz Melodic Minor

Fingering #1

Fingering #2

Fingering #3

Fingering #4

Exercise #43: Ascending 4ths in C Harmonic Minor

Fingering #1

Fingering #2

Fingering #3

Fingering #4

Exercise #44: Descending 4ths in C Major

Fingering #1

Fingering #2

Fingering #3

Fingering #4

Exercise #45: Descending 4ths in C Jazz Melodic Minor

Fingering #1

Fingering #2

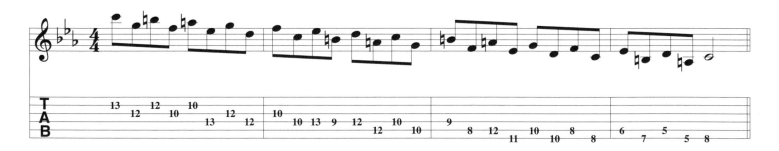

Fingering #3

Fingering #4

Exercise #46: Descending 4ths in C Harmonic Minor

Fingering #1

Fingering #2

Fingering #3

Fingering #4

Exercise #47: Descending 4ths in C Major

Fingering #1

Fingering #2

Fingering #3

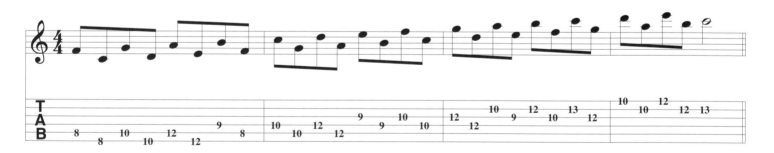

Fingering #4

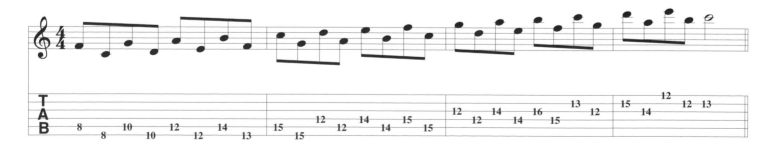

Exercise #48: Descending 4ths in C Jazz Melodic Minor

Fingering #1

Fingering #2

Fingering #3

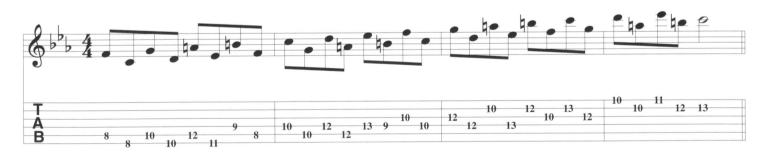

Fingering #4

Exercise #49: Descending 4ths in C Harmonic Minor

Fingering #1

Fingering #2

Fingering #3

Fingering #4

Exercise #50: Ascending 4ths in C Major

Fingering #1

Fingering #2

Fingering #3

Fingering #4

Exercise #51: Ascending 4ths in C Jazz Melodic Minor

Fingering #1

Fingering #2

Fingering #3

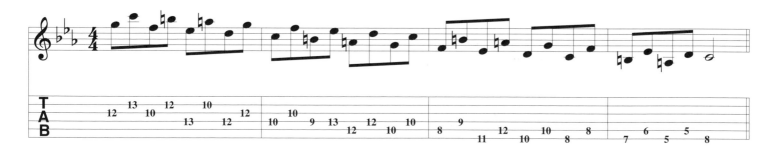

Fingering #4

Exercise #52: Ascending 4ths in C Harmonic Minor

Fingering #1

Fingering #2

Fingering #3

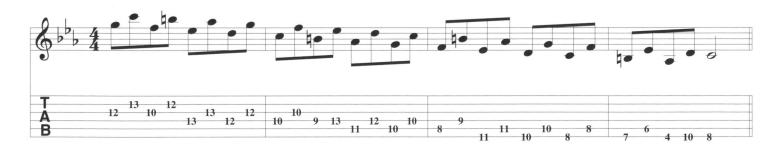

Fingering #4

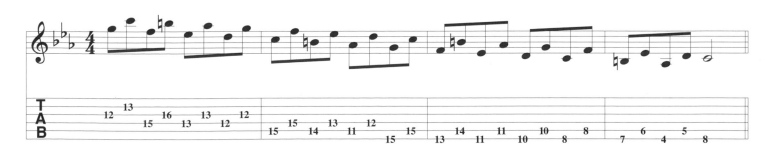

Exercise #53: Ascending 5ths in C Major

Fingering #1

Fingering #2

Fingering #3

Fingering #4

Exercise #54: Ascending 5ths in C Jazz Melodic Minor

Fingering #1

Fingering #2

Fingering #3

Fingering #4

Exercise #55: Ascending 5ths in C Harmonic Minor

Fingering #1

Fingering #2

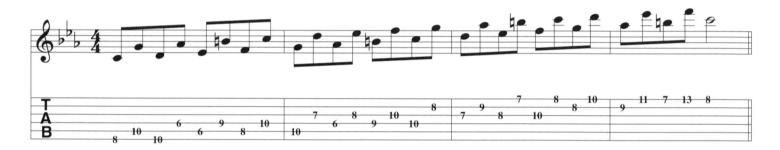

Fingering #3

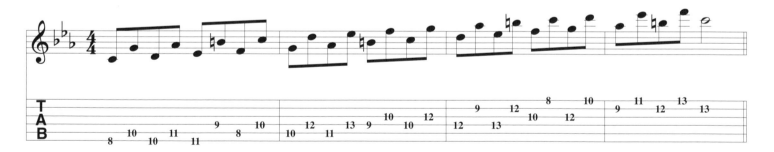

Fingering #4

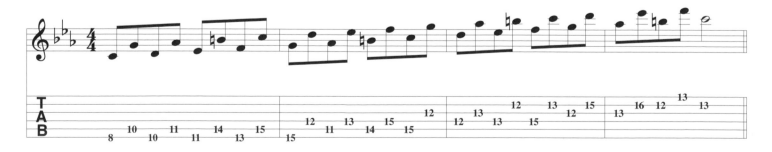

Exercise #56: Descending 5ths in C Major

Fingering #1

Fingering #2

Fingering #3

Fingering #4

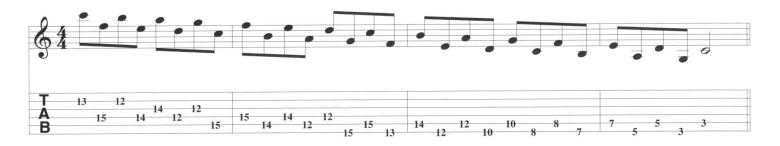

Exercise #57: Descending 5ths in C Jazz Melodic Minor

Fingering #1

Fingering #2

Fingering #3

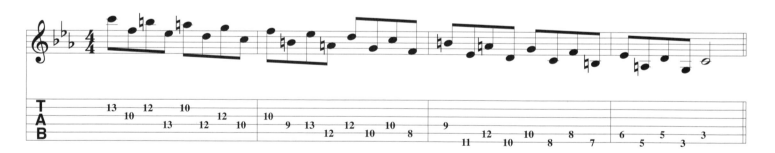

Fingering #4

Exercise #58: Descending 5ths in C Harmonic Minor

Fingering #1

Fingering #2

Fingering #3

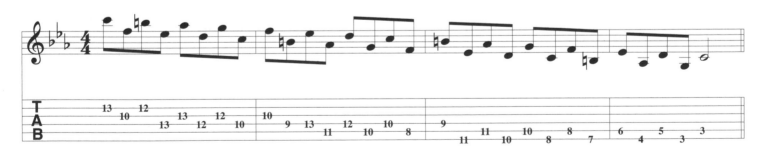

Fingering #4

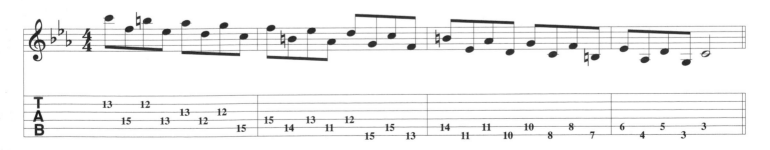

Exercise #59: Descending 5ths in C Major

Fingering #1

Fingering #2

Fingering #3

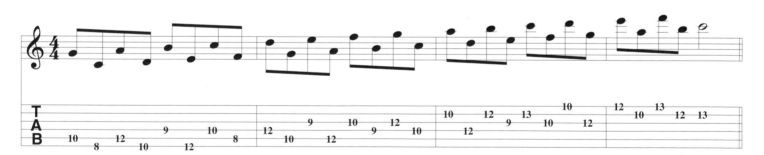

Fingering #4

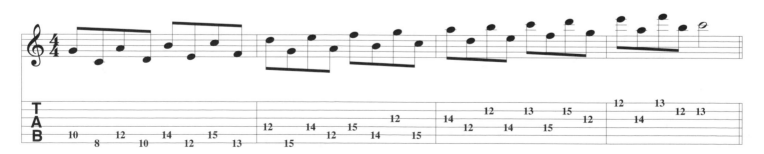

Exercise #60: Descending 5ths in C Jazz Melodic Minor

Fingering #1

Fingering #2

Fingering #3

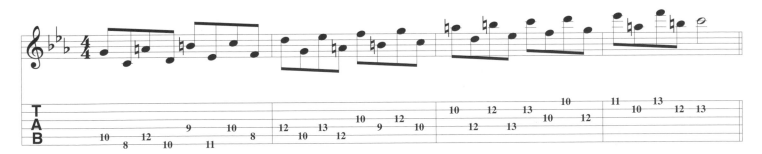

Fingering #4

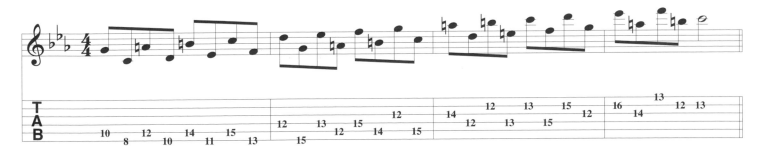

Exercise #61: Descending 5ths in C Harmonic Minor

Fingering #1

Fingering #2

Fingering #3

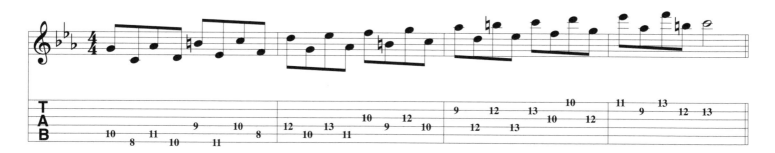

Fingering #4

Exercise #62: Ascending 5ths in C Major

Fingering #1

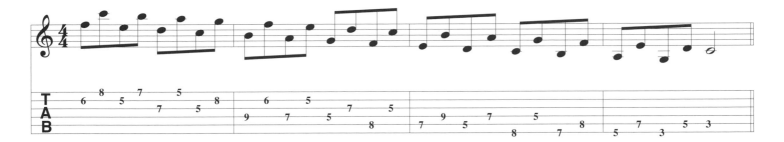

Fingering #2

Fingering #3

Fingering #4

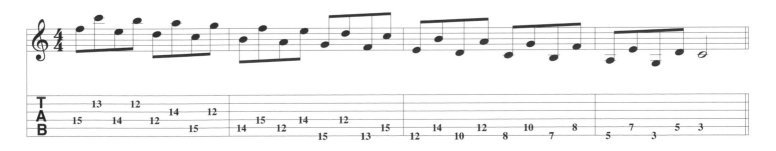

Exercise #63: Ascending 5ths in C Jazz Melodic Minor

Fingering #1

Fingering #2

Fingering #3

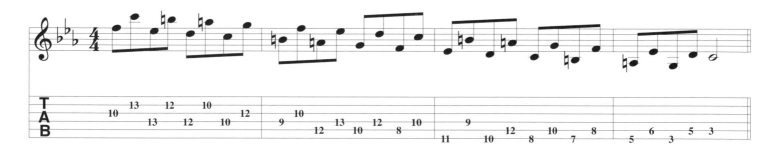

Fingering #4

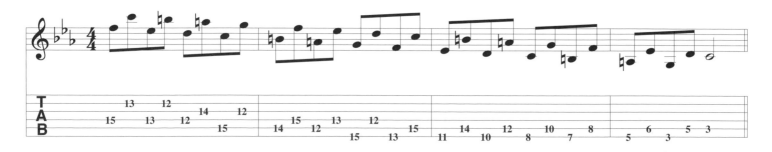

Exercise #64: Ascending 5ths in C Harmonic Minor

Fingering #1

Fingering #2

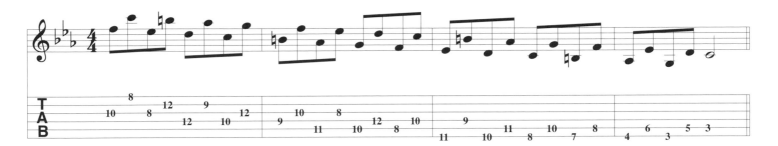

Fingering #3

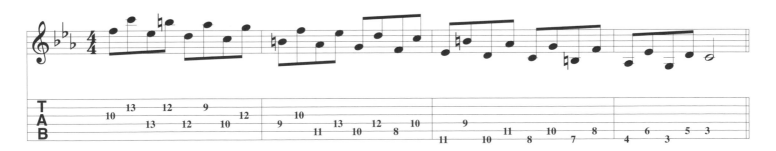

Fingering #4

Exercise #65: Ascending 6ths in C Major

Fingering #1

Fingering #2

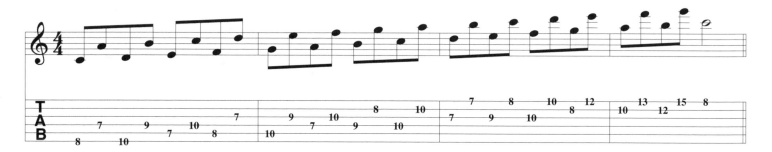

Fingering #3

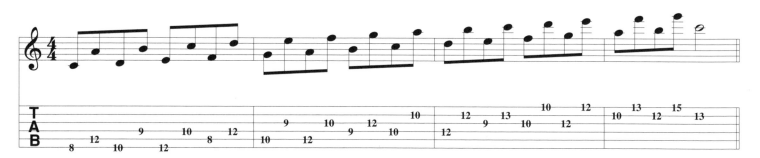

Fingering #4

Exercise #66: Ascending 6ths in C Jazz Melodic Minor

Fingering #1

Fingering #2

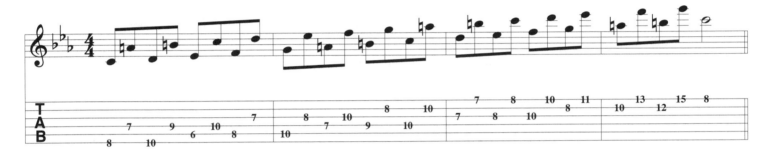

Fingering #3

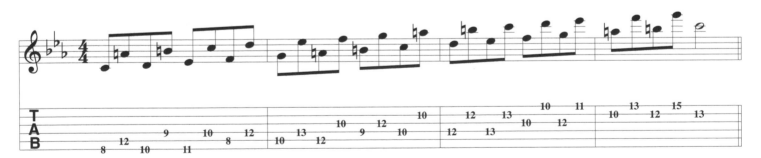

Fingering #4

Exercise #67: Ascending 6ths in C Harmonic Minor

Fingering #1

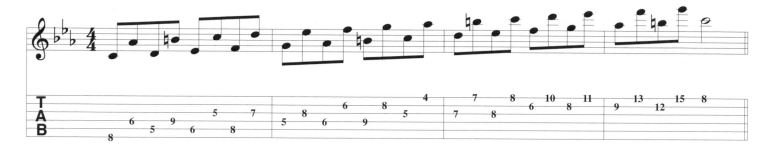

Fingering #2

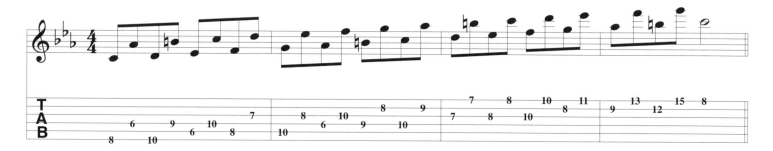

Fingering #3

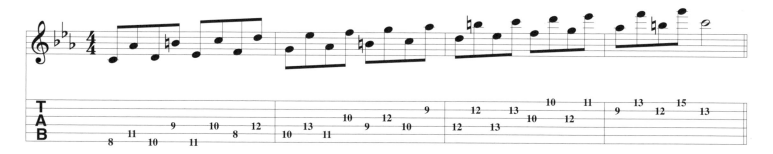

Fingering #4

Exercise #68: Descending 6ths in C Major

Fingering #1

Fingering #2

Fingering #3

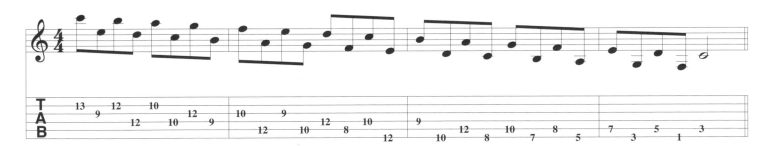

Fingering #4

Exercise #69: Descending 6ths in C Jazz Melodic Minor

Fingering #1

Fingering #2

Fingering #3

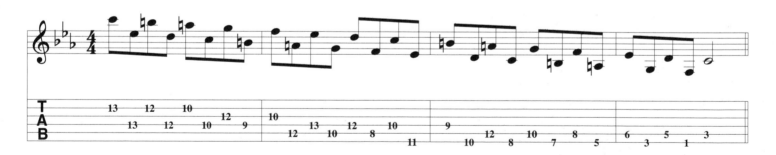

Fingering #4

Exercise #70: Descending 6ths in C Harmonic Minor

Fingering #1

Fingering #2

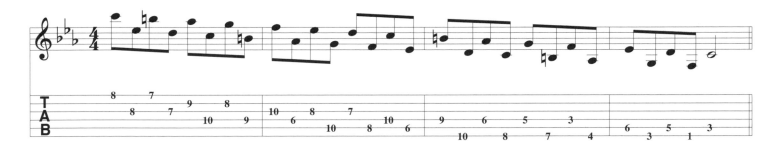

Fingering #3

Fingering #4

Exercise #71: Descending 6ths in C Major

Fingering #1

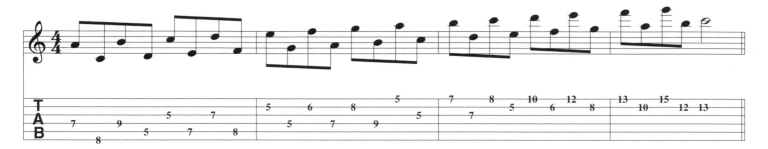

Fingering #2

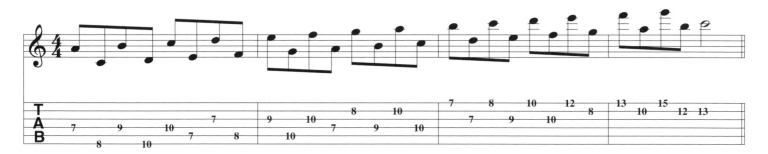

Fingering #3

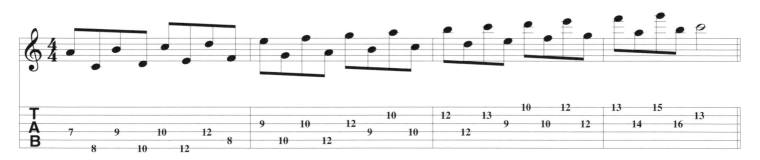

Fingering #4

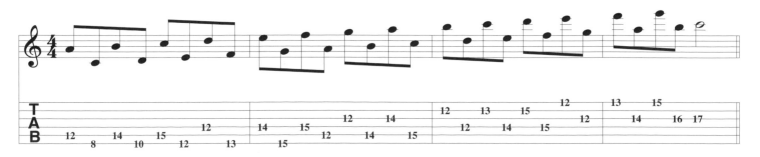

Exercise #72: Descending 6ths in C Jazz Melodic Minor

Fingering #1

Fingering #2

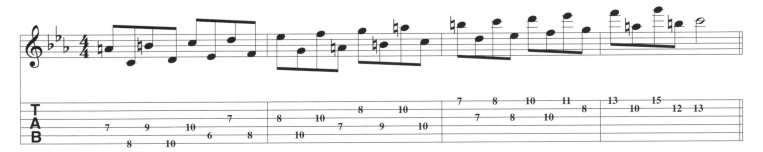

Fingering #3

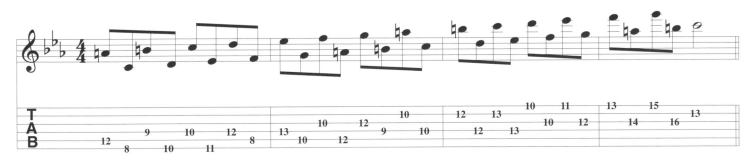

Fingering #4

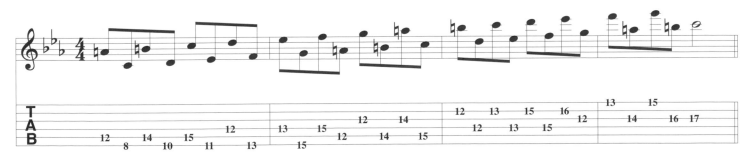

Exercise #73: Descending 6ths in C Harmonic Minor

Fingering #1

Fingering #2

Fingering #3

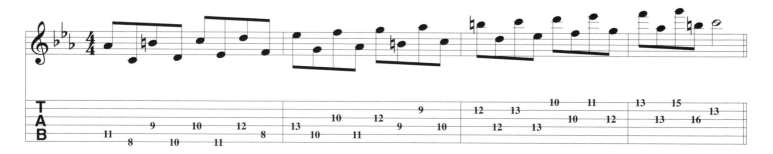

Fingering #4

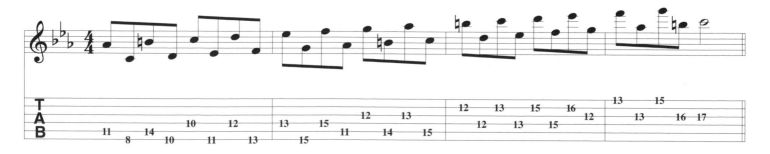

Exercise #74: Ascending 6ths in C Major

Fingering #1

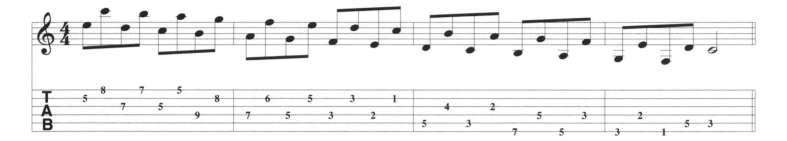

Fingering #2

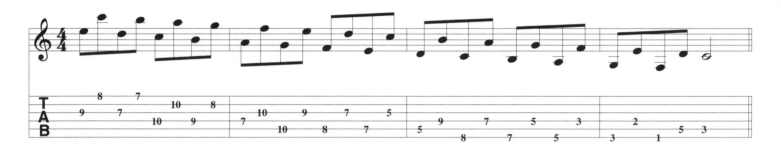

Fingering #3

Fingering #4

Exercise #75: Ascending 6ths in C Jazz Melodic Minor

Fingering #1

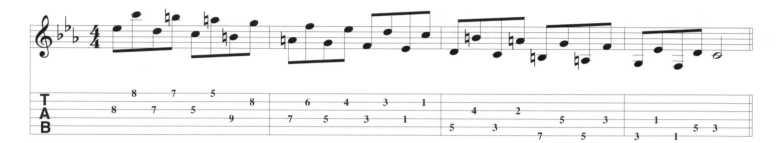

Fingering #2

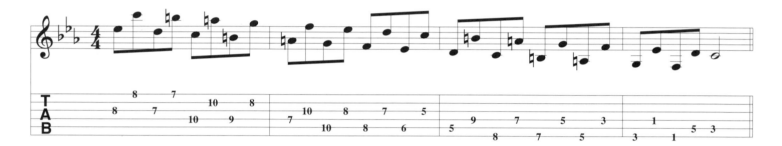

Fingering #3

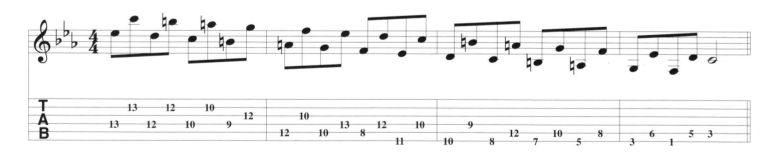

Fingering #4

Exercise #76: Ascending 7ths in C Major

Fingering #1

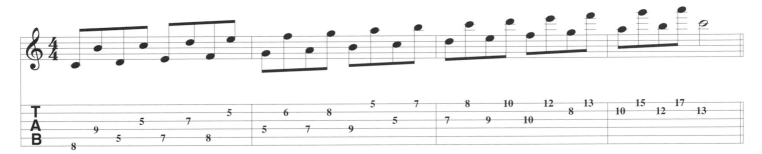

Fingering #2

Fingering #3

Fingering #4

Exercise #77: Ascending 7ths in C Jazz Melodic Minor

Fingering #1

Fingering #2

Fingering #3

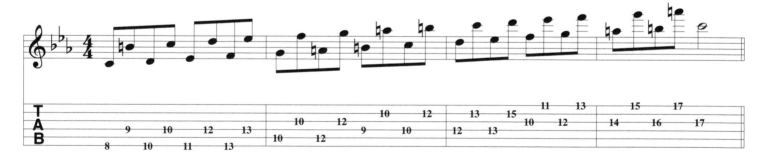

Fingering #4

Exercise #78: Ascending 7ths in C Harmonic Minor

Fingering #1

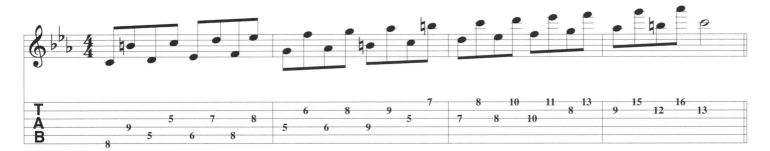

Fingering #2

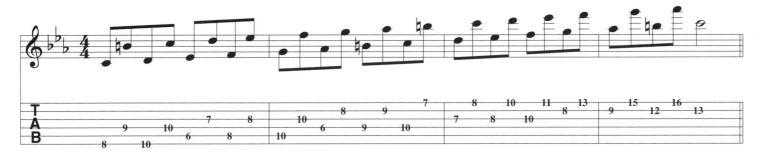

Fingering #3

Fingering #4

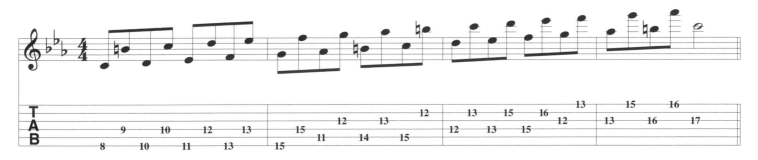

Exercise #79: Descending 7ths in C Major

Fingering #1

Fingering #2

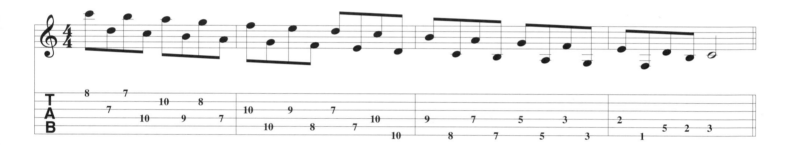

Fingering #3

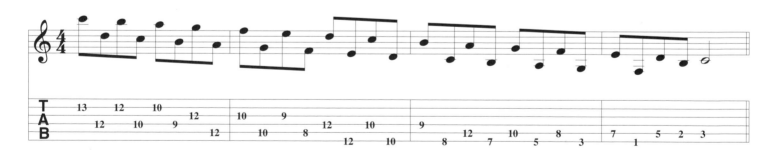

Fingering #4

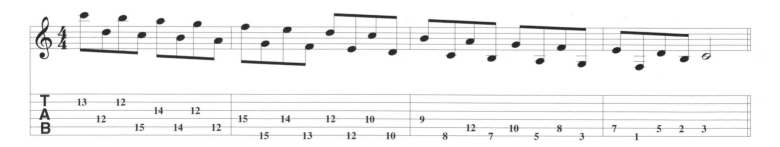

Exercise #80: Descending 7ths in C Jazz Melodic Minor

Fingering #1

Fingering #2

Fingering #3

Fingering #4

Exercise #81: Descending 7ths in C Harmonic Minor

Fingering #1

Fingering #2

Fingering #3

Fingering #4

Exercise #82: Descending 7ths in C Major

Fingering #1

Fingering #2

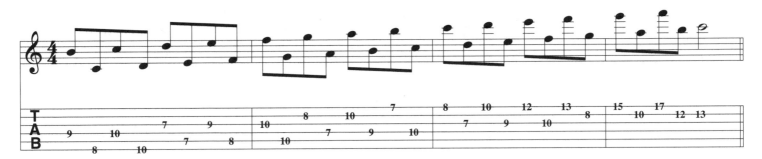

Fingering #3

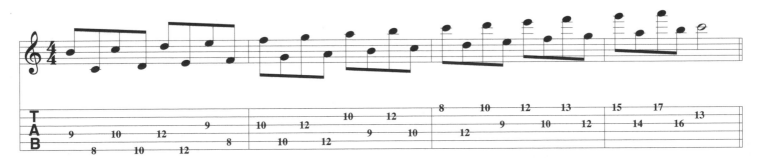

Fingering #4

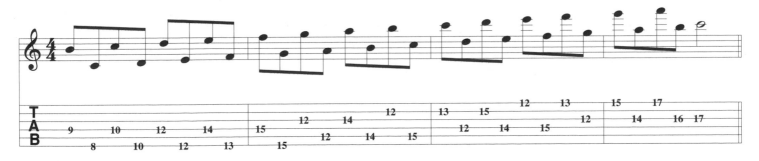

Exercise #83: Descending 7ths in C Jazz Melodic Minor

Fingering #1

Fingering #2

Fingering #3

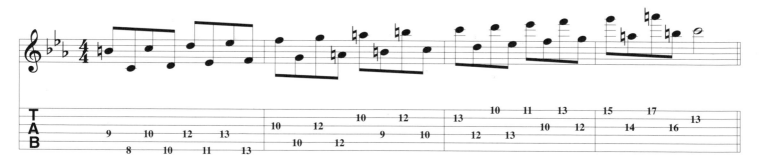

Fingering #4

Exercise #84: Descending 7ths in C Harmonic Minor

Fingering #1

Fingering #2

Fingering #3

Fingering #4

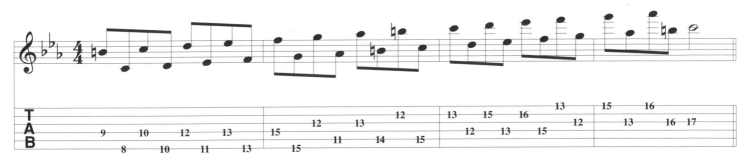

Exercise #85: Ascending 7ths in C Major

Fingering #1

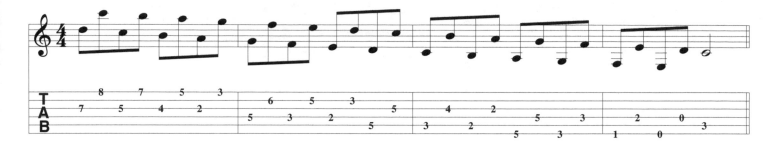

Fingering #2

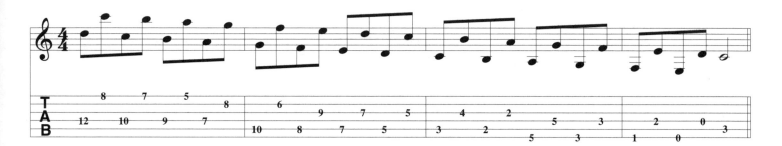

Fingering #3

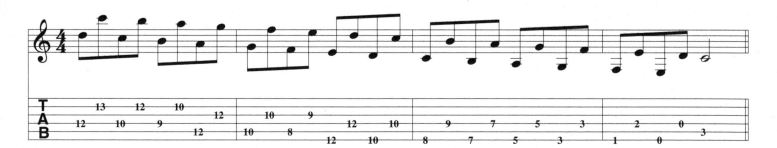

Fingering #4

Exercise #86: Ascending 7ths in C Jazz Melodic Minor

Fingering #1

Fingering #2

Fingering #3

Fingering #4

Exercise #87: Ascending 7ths in C Harmonic Minor

Fingering #1

Fingering #2

Fingering #3

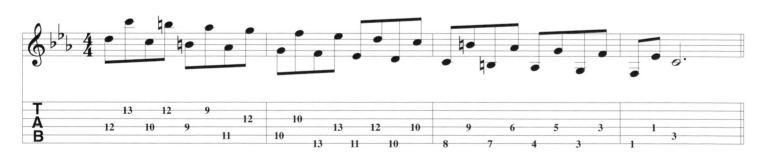

Fingering #4

Exercise #88: C Arpeggio

Fingering #1

Fingering #2

Fingering #3

Fingering #4

Exercise #89: Cm Arpeggio

Fingering #1

Fingering #2

Fingering #3

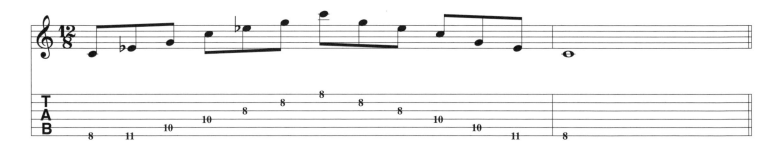

Fingering #4

Exercise #90: Caug Arpeggio

Fingering #1

Fingering #2

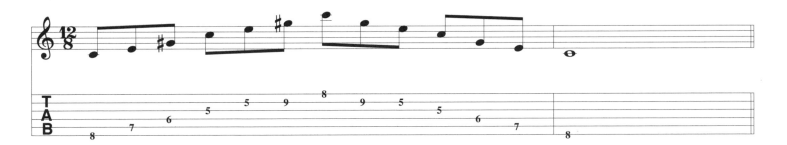

Fingering #3

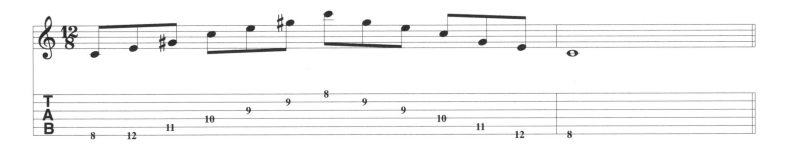

Fingering #4

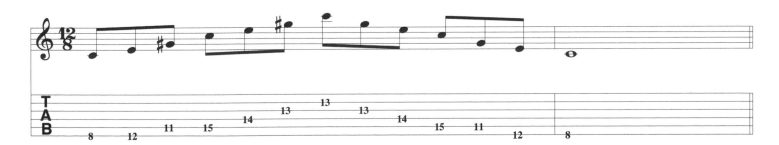

Exercise #91: Cdim Arpeggio

Fingering #1

Fingering #2

Fingering #3

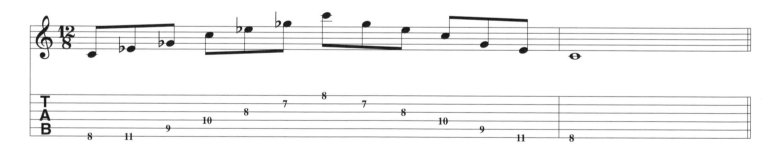

Fingering #4

Exercise #92: Csus4 Arpeggio

Fingering #1

Fingering #2

Fingering #3

Fingering #4

Exercise #93: Csus2 Arpeggio

Fingering #1

Fingering #2

Fingering #3

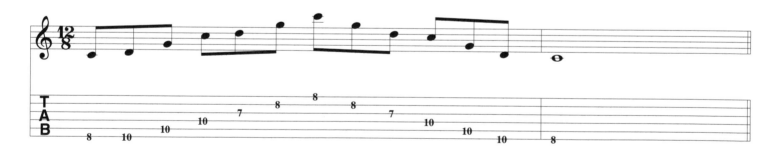

Fingering #4

Exercise #94: Cadd9 Arpeggio

Fingering #1

Fingering #2

Fingering #3

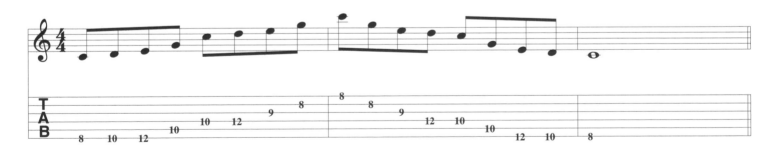

Fingering #4

Exercise #95: Cm(add9) Arpeggio

Fingering #1

Fingering #2

Fingering #3

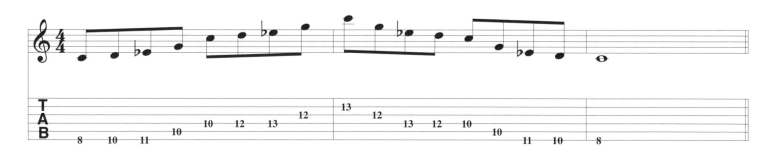

Fingering #4

Exercise #96: C6 Arpeggio

Fingering #1

Fingering #2

Fingering #3

Fingering #4

Exercise #97: Cm6 Arpeggio

Fingering #1

Fingering #2

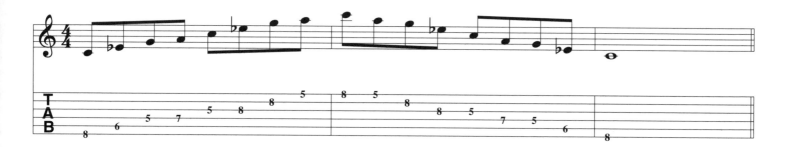

Fingering #3

Fingering #4

Exercise #98: Cmaj7 Arpeggio

Fingering #1

Fingering #2

Fingering #3

Fingering #4

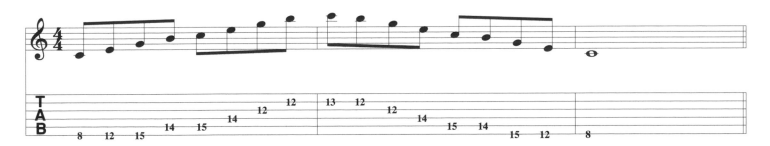

Exercise #99: C7 Arpeggio

Fingering #1

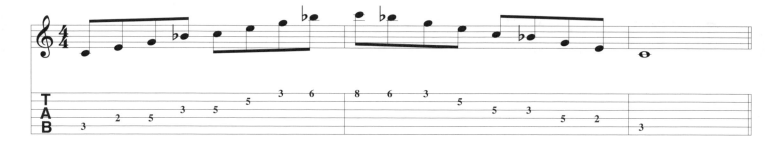

Fingering #2

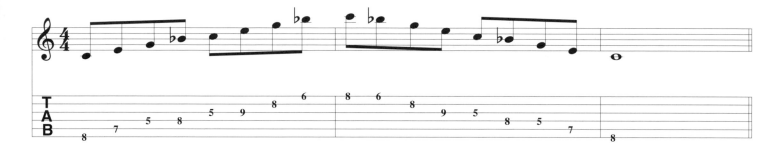

Fingering #3

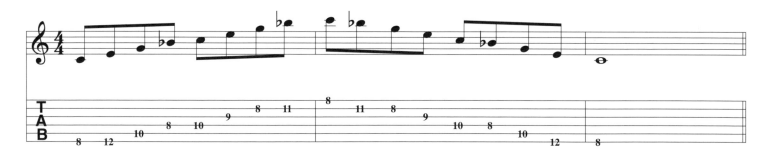

Fingering #4

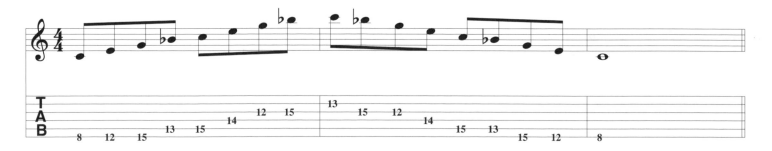

Exercise #100: Cm7 Arpeggio

Fingering #1

Fingering #2

Fingering #3

Fingering #4

Exercise #101: Cmaj7#5 Arpeggio

Fingering #1

Fingering #2

Fingering #3

Fingering #4

Exercise #102: Cmaj7♭5 Arpeggio

Fingering #1

Fingering #2

Fingering #3

Fingering #4

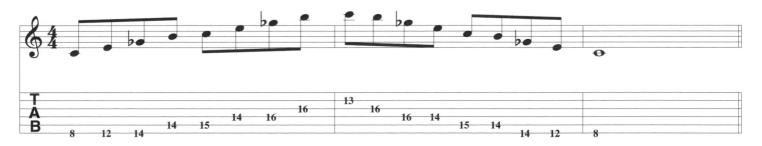

Exercise #103: C7#5 Arpeggio

Fingering #1

Fingering #2

Fingering #3

Fingering #4

Exercise #104: C7♭5 Arpeggio

Fingering #1

Fingering #2

Fingering #3

Fingering #4

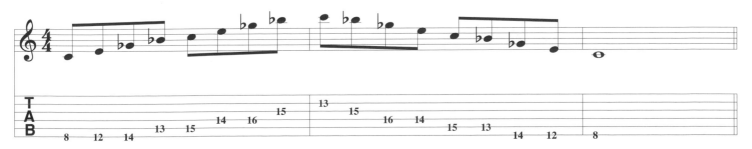

Exercise #105: Cm7♭5 Arpeggio

Fingering #1

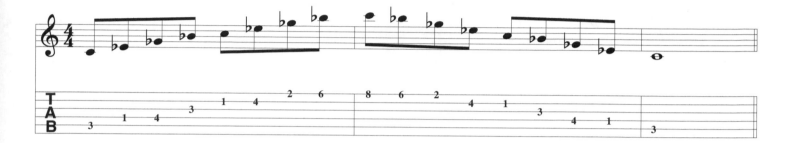

Fingering #2

Fingering #3

Fingering #4

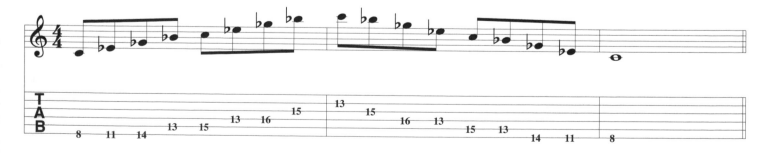

Exercise #106: Cm(maj7) Arpeggio

Fingering #1

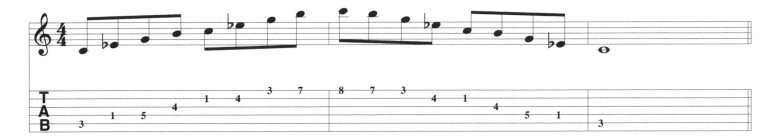

Fingering #2

Fingering #3

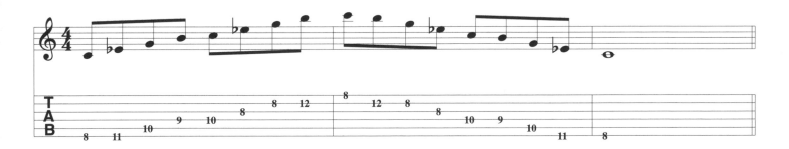

Fingering #4

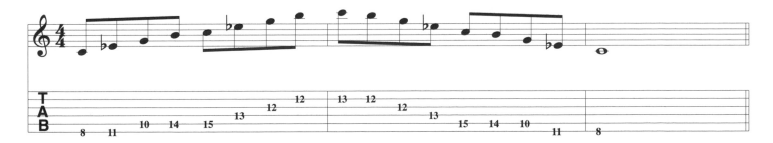

Exercise #107: Cdim7 Arpeggio

Fingering #1

Fingering #2

Fingering #3

Fingering #4

Exercise #108: Cm(maj7)♭5 Arpeggio

Fingering #1

Fingering #2

Fingering #3

Fingering #4

Exercise #109: C Arpeggio Sequence

Fingering #1

Fingering #2

Fingering #3

Fingering #4

Exercise #110: Cm Arpeggio Sequence

Fingering #1

Fingering #2

Fingering #3

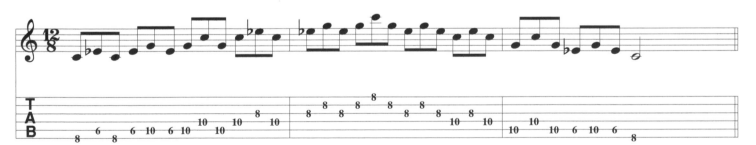

Fingering #4

Exercise #111: Caug Arpeggio Sequence

Fingering #1

Fingering #2

Fingering #3

Fingering #4

Exercise #112: Cdim Arpeggio Sequence

Fingering #1

Fingering #2

Fingering #3

Fingering #4

Exercise #113: Csus4 Arpeggio Sequence

Fingering #1

Fingering #2

Fingering #3

Fingering #4

Exercise #114: Csus2 Arpeggio Sequence

Fingering #1

Fingering #2

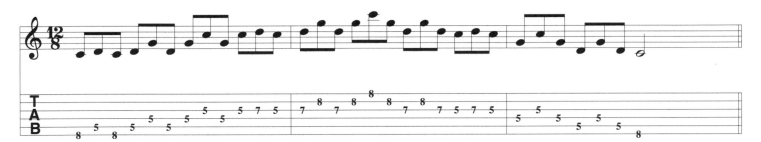

Fingering #3

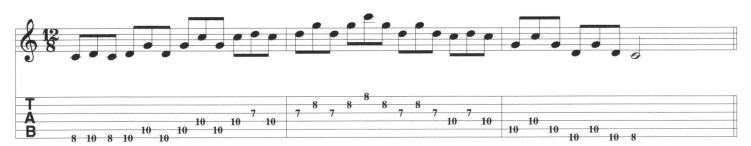

Fingering #4

Exercise #115: Cadd9 Arpeggio Sequence

Fingering #1

Fingering #2

Exercise #115: Cadd9 Arpeggio Sequence

Fingering #3

Fingering #4

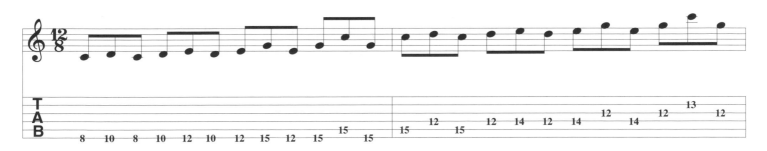

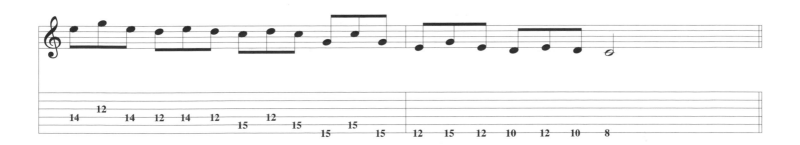

Exercise #116: Cm(add9) Arpeggio Sequence

Fingering #1

Fingering #2

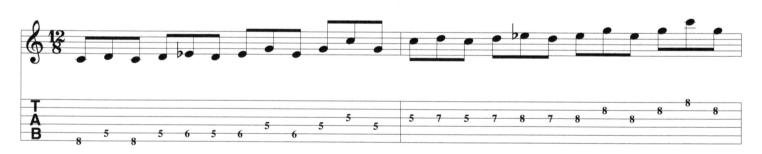

Exercise #116: Cm(add9) Arpeggio Sequence

Fingering #3

Fingering #4

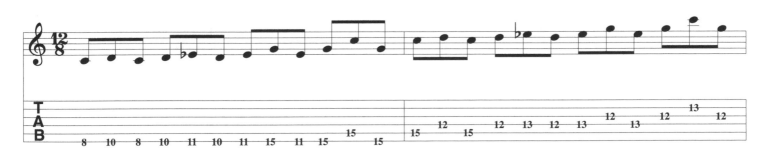

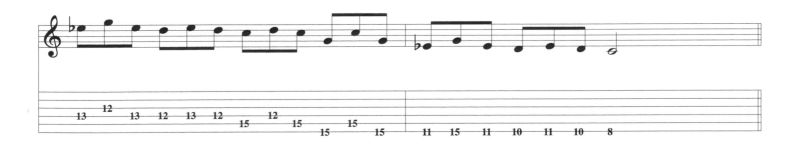

Exercise #117: C6 Arpeggio Sequence

Fingering #1

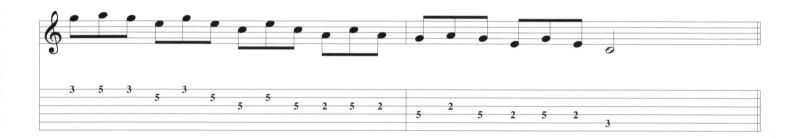

Fingering #2

Exercise #117: C6 Arpeggio Sequence

Fingering #3

Fingering #4

Exercise #118: Cm6 Arpeggio Sequence

Fingering #1

Fingering #2

Exercise #118: Cm6 Arpeggio Sequence

Fingering #3

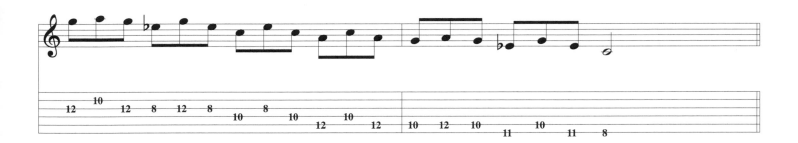

Fingering #4

Exercise #119: Cmaj7 Arpeggio Sequence

Fingering #1

Fingering #2

Exercise #119: Cmaj7 Arpeggio Sequence

Fingering #3

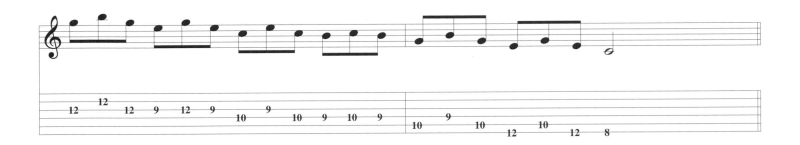

Fingering #4

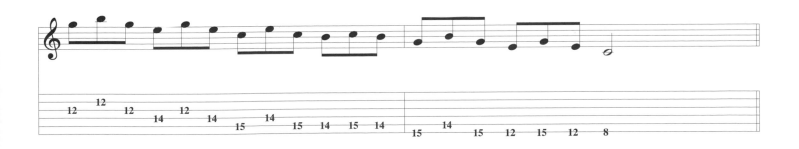

Exercise #120: C7 Arpeggio Sequence

Fingering #1

Fingering #2

Exercise #120: C7 Arpeggio Sequence

Fingering #3

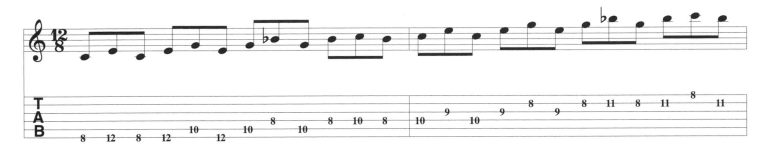

Fingering #4

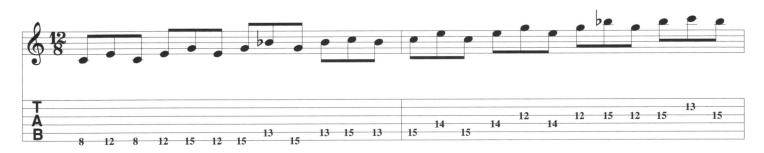

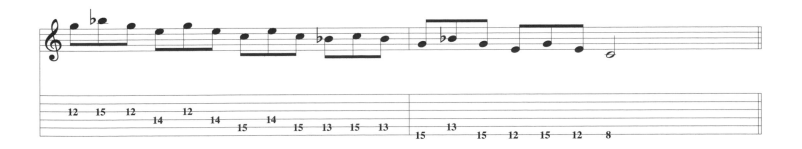

Exercise #121: Cm7 Arpeggio Sequence

Fingering #1

Fingering #2

Exercise #121: Cm7 Arpeggio Sequence

Fingering #3

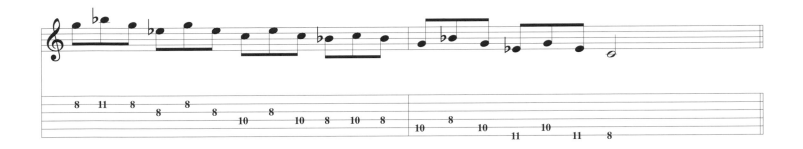

Fingering #4

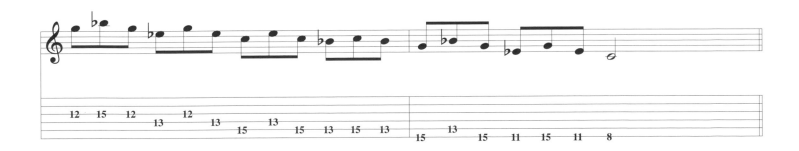

Exercise #122: Cmaj7#5 Arpeggio Sequence

Fingering #1

Fingering #2

Exercise #122: Cmaj7♯5 Arpeggio Sequence

Fingering #3

Fingering #4

Exercise #123: Cmaj7♭5 Arpeggio Sequence

Fingering #1

Fingering #2

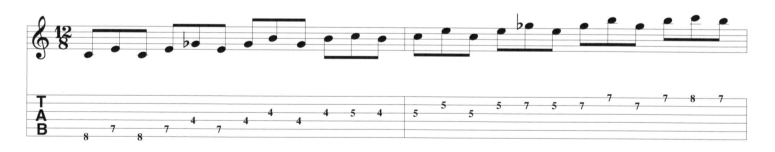

Exercise #123: Cmaj7♭5 Arpeggio Sequence

Fingering #3

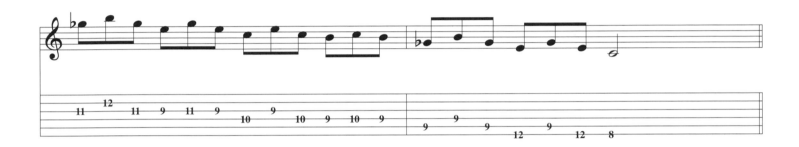

Fingering #4

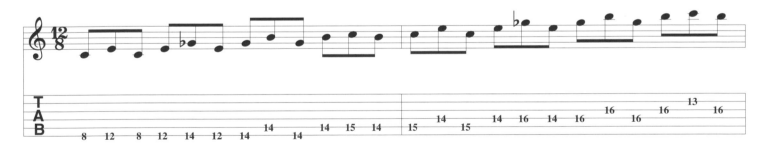

Exercise #124: C7#5 Arpeggio Sequence

Fingering #1

Fingering #2

Exercise #124: C7#5 Arpeggio Sequence

Fingering #3

Fingering #4

Exercise #125: C7♭5 Arpeggio Sequence

Fingering #1

Fingering #2

Exercise #125: C7♭5 Arpeggio Sequence

Fingering #3

Fingering #4

Exercise #126: Cm7♭5 Arpeggio Sequence

Fingering #1

Fingering #2

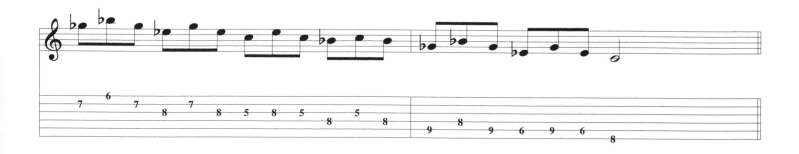

Exercise #126: Cm7♭5 Arpeggio Sequence

Fingering #3

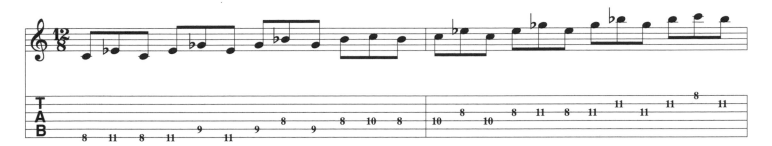

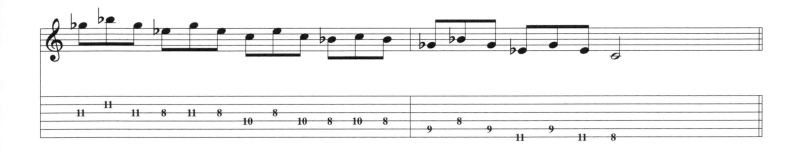

Fingering #4

Exercise #127: Cm(maj7) Arpeggio Sequence

Fingering #1

Fingering #2

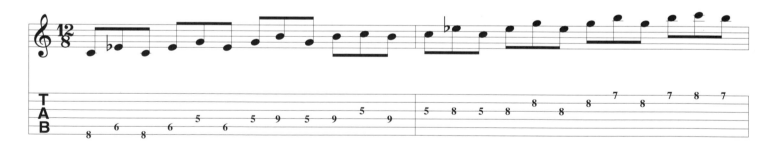

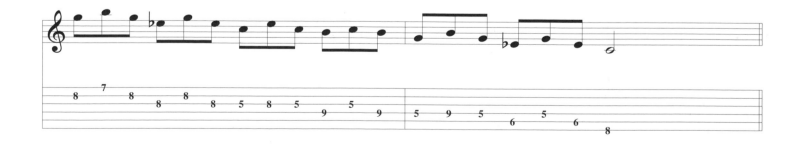

Exercise #127: Cm(maj7) Arpeggio Sequence

Fingering #3

Fingering #4

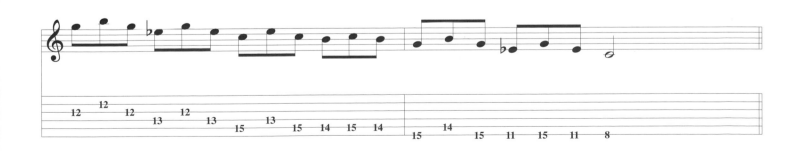

Exercise #128: Cdim7 Arpeggio Sequence

Fingering #1

Fingering #2

Exercise #128: Cdim7 Arpeggio Sequence

Fingering #3

Fingering #4

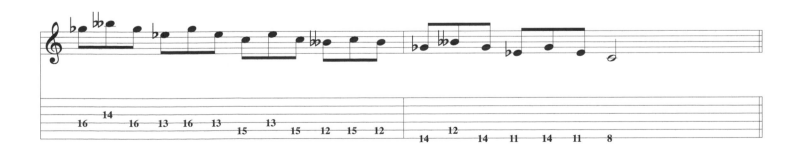

Exercise #129: Cm(maj7)♭5 Arpeggio Sequence

Fingering #1

Fingering #2

Exercise #129: Cm(maj7)♭5 Arpeggio Sequence

Fingering #3

Fingering #4

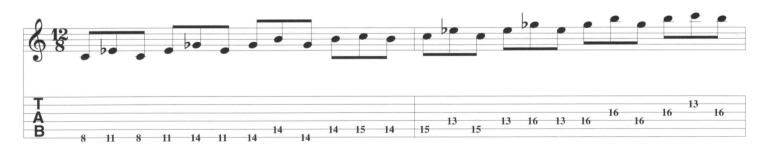

Exercise #130: C Arpeggio Sequence

Fingering #1

Fingering #2

Fingering #3

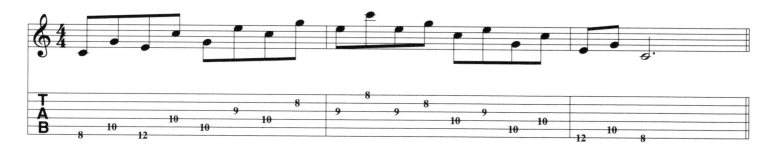

Fingering #4

Exercise #131: Cm Arpeggio Sequence

Fingering #1

Fingering #2

Fingering #3

Fingering #4

Exercise #132: Caug Arpeggio Sequence

Fingering #1

Fingering #2

Fingering #3

Fingering #4

Exercise #133: Cdim Arpeggio Sequence

Fingering #1

Fingering #2

Fingering #3

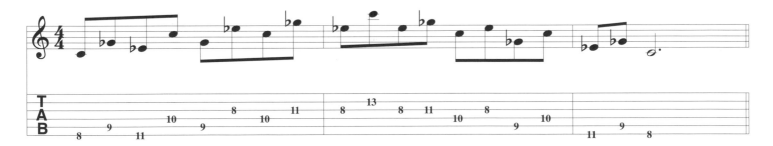

Fingering #4

Exercise #134: Csus4 Arpeggio Sequence

Fingering #1

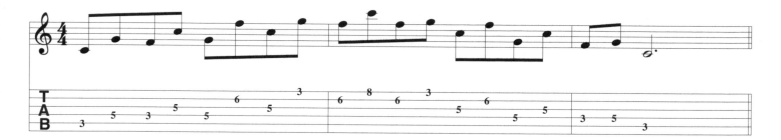

Fingering #2

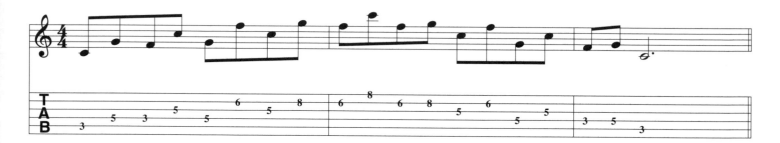

Fingering #3

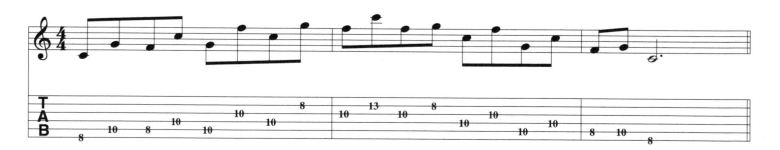

Fingering #4

Exercise #135: Csus2 Arpeggio Sequence

Fingering #1

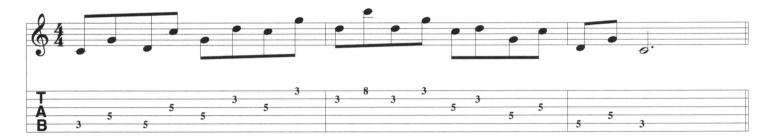

Fingering #2

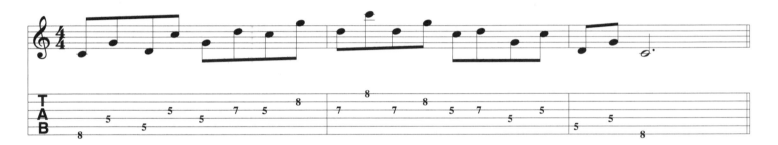

Fingering #3

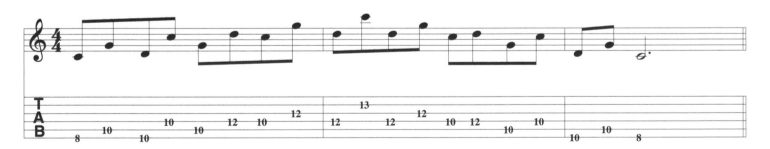

Fingering #4

Exercise #136: Cadd9 Arpeggio Sequence

Fingering #1

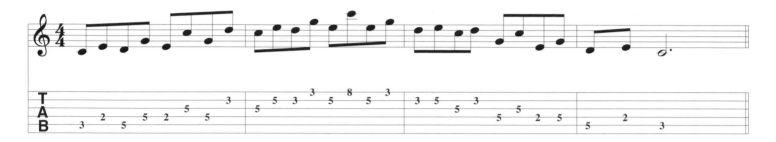

Fingering #2

Fingering #3

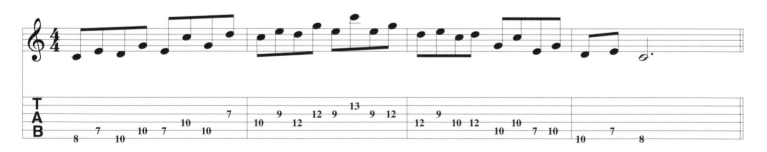

Fingering #4

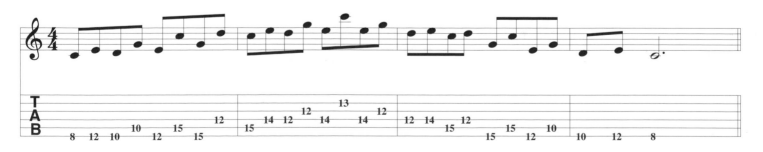

Exercise #137: Cm(add9) Arpeggio Sequence

Fingering #1

Fingering #2

Fingering #3

Fingering #4

Exercise #138: C6 Arpeggio Sequence

Fingering #1

Fingering #2

Fingering #3

Fingering #4

Exercise #139: Cm6 Arpeggio Sequence

Fingering #1

Fingering #2

Fingering #3

Fingering #4

Exercise #140: Cmaj7 Arpeggio Sequence

Fingering #1

Fingering #2

Fingering #3

Fingering #4

Exercise #141: C7 Arpeggio Sequence

Fingering #1

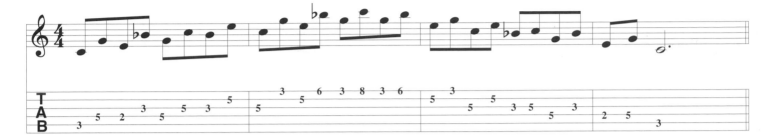

Fingering #2

Fingering #3

Fingering #4

Exercise #142: Cm7 Arpeggio Sequence

Fingering #1

Fingering #2

Fingering #3

Fingering #4

Exercise #143: Cmaj7♯5 Arpeggio Sequence

Fingering #1

Fingering #2

Fingering #3

Fingering #4

Exercise #144: Cmaj7♭5 Arpeggio Sequence

Fingering #1

Fingering #2

Fingering #3

Fingering #4

Exercise #145: C7♯5 Arpeggio Sequence

Fingering #1

Fingering #2

Fingering #3

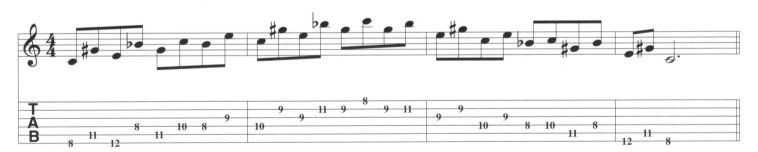

Fingering #4

Exercise #146: C7♭5 Arpeggio Sequence

Fingering #1

Fingering #2

Fingering #3

Fingering #4

Exercise #147: Cm7♭5 Arpeggio Sequence

Fingering #1

Fingering #2

Fingering #3

Fingering #4

Exercise #148: Cm(maj7) Arpeggio Sequence

Fingering #1

Fingering #2

Fingering #3

Fingering #4

Exercise #149: Cdim7 Arpeggio Sequence

Fingering #1

Fingering #2

Fingering #3

Fingering #4

Exercise #150: Cm(maj7)♭5 Arpeggio Sequence

Fingering #1

Fingering #2

Fingering #3

Fingering #4

Exercise #151: Diatonic Arpeggio Sequence in C Major

Fingering #1

Fingering #2

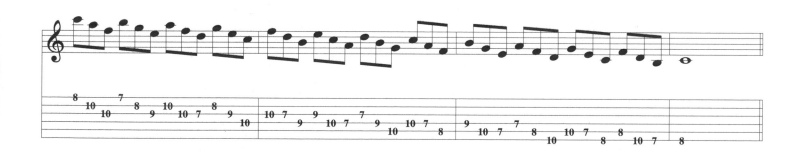

Exercise #151: Diatonic Arpeggio Sequence in C Major

Fingering #3

Fingering #4

Exercise #152: Diatonic Arpeggio Sequence in C Major

Fingering #1

Fingering #2

Exercise #152: Diatonic Arpeggio Sequence in C Major

Fingering #3

Fingering #4

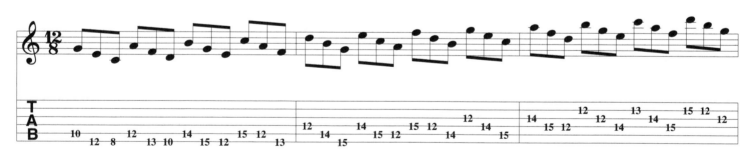

Exercise #153: Diatonic Arpeggio Sequence in C Major

Fingering #1

Fingering #2

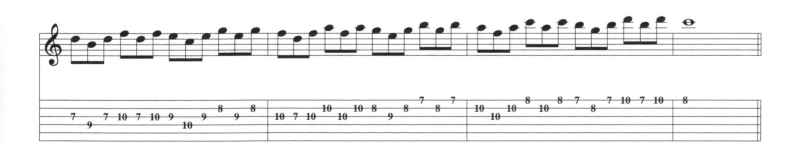

Exercise #153: Diatonic Arpeggio Sequence in C Major

Fingering #3

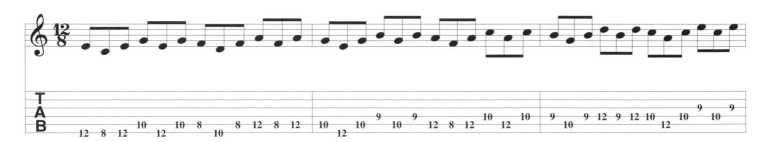

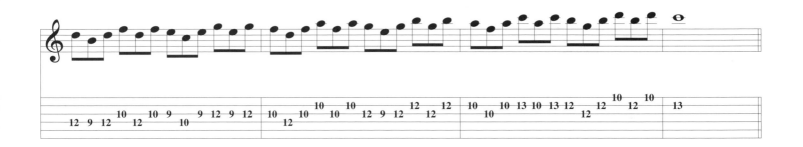

Fingering #4

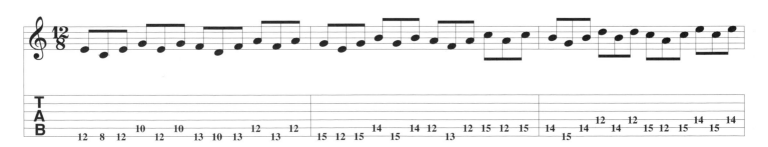

Exercise #154: Diatonic Arpeggio Sequence in C Major

Fingering #1

Fingering #2

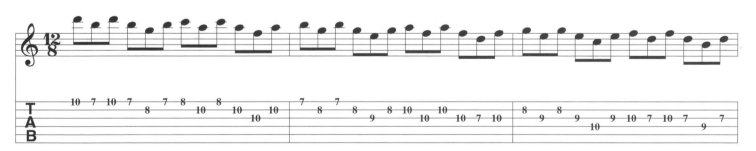

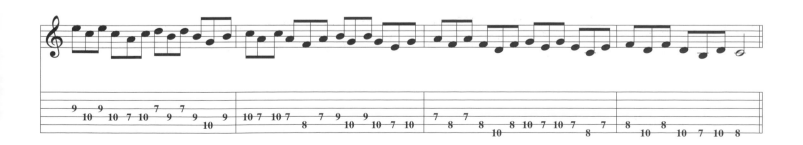

Exercise #154: Diatonic Arpeggio Sequence in C Major

Fingering #3

Fingering #4

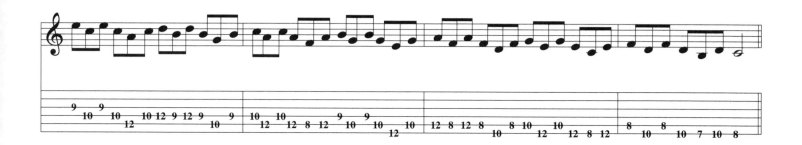

Exercise #155: Diatonic Arpeggio Sequence in C Major

Fingering #1

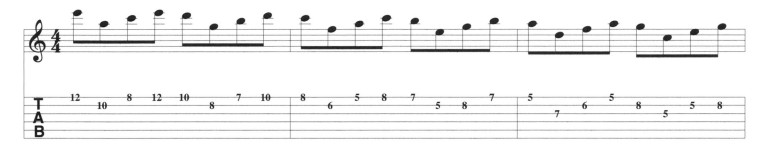

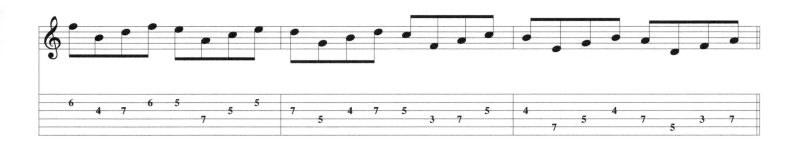

Fingering #2

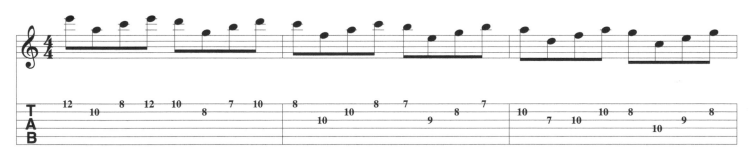

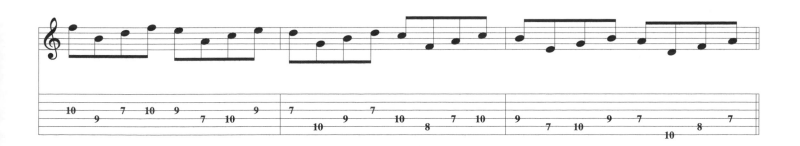

Exercise #155: Diatonic Arpeggio Sequence in C Major

Fingering #3

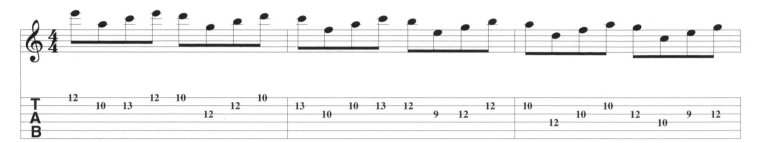

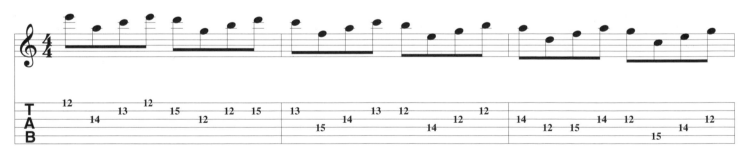

Fingering #4

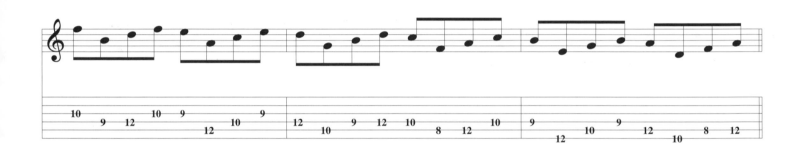

Exercise #156: Diatonic Arpeggio Sequence in C Major

Fingering #1

Fingering #2

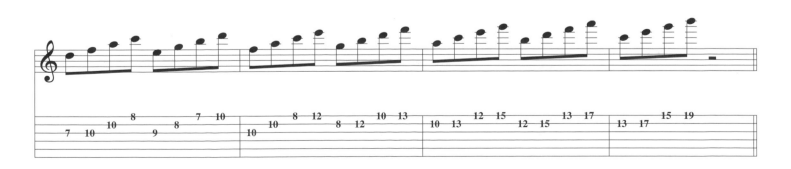

Exercise #156: Diatonic Arpeggio Sequence in C Major

Fingering #3

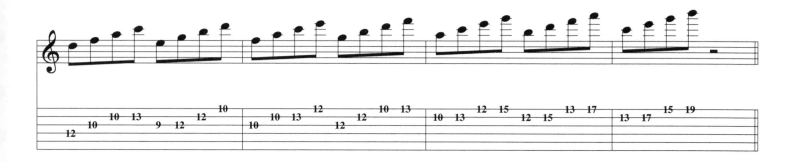

Fingering #4

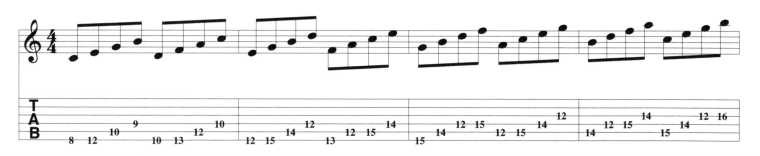

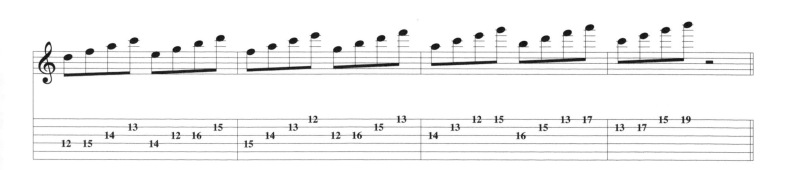

Exercise #157: Diatonic Arpeggio Sequence in C Major

Fingering #1

Fingering #2

Fingering #3

Fingering #4

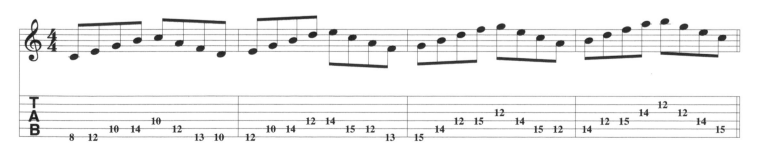

Exercise #158: Linear Diatonic Arpeggios in C Major

#1

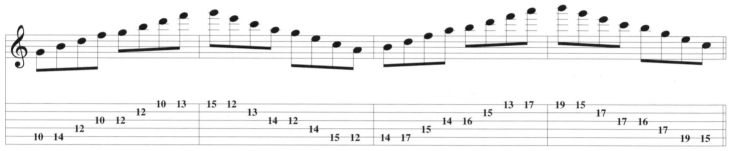

#2

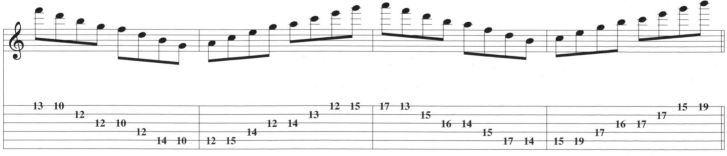

Exercise #159: Linear Diatonic Arpeggios in C Major

#1

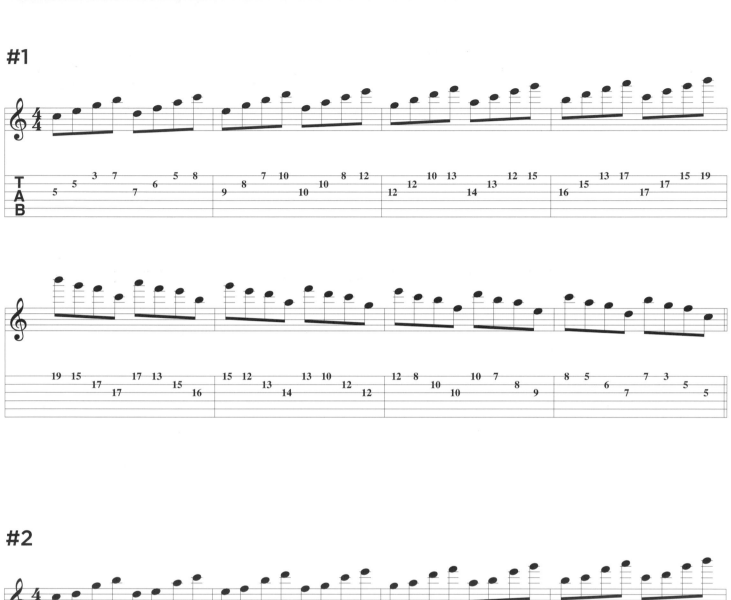

#2

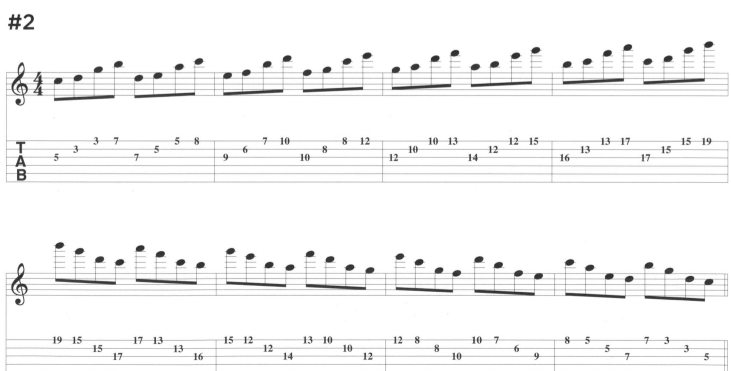

J.S. Bach Sonata #5 Allegro Assai

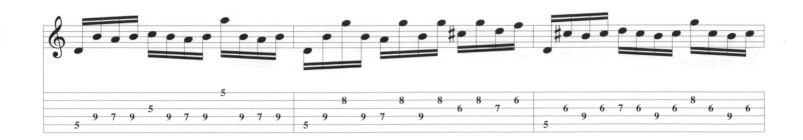

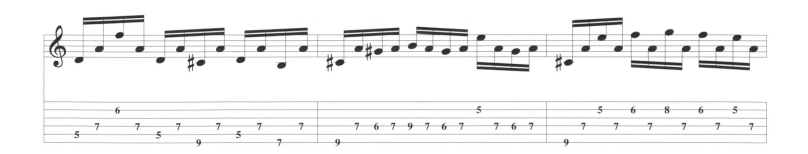

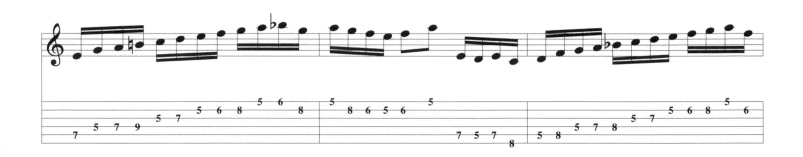

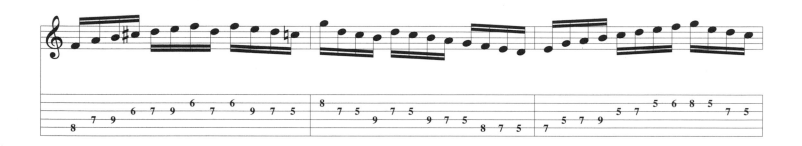

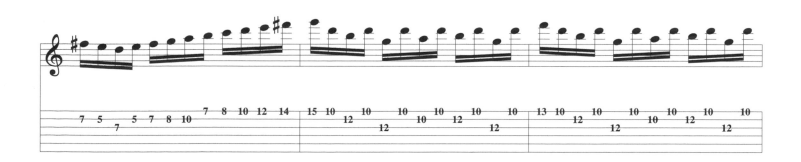

Paganini Moto Perpetuo

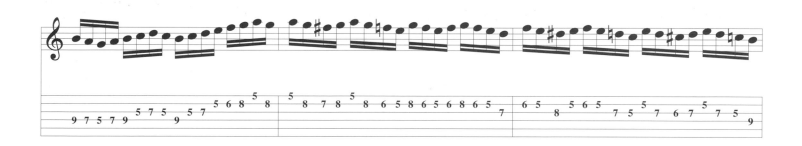

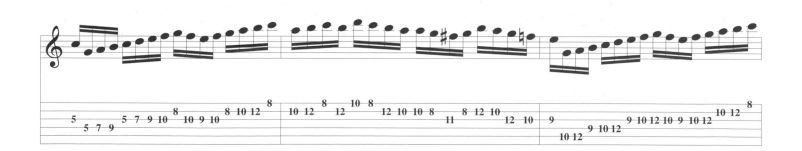

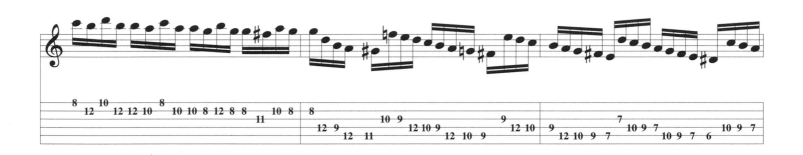

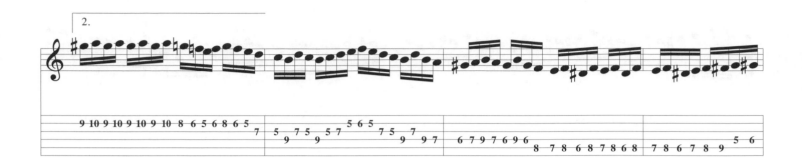

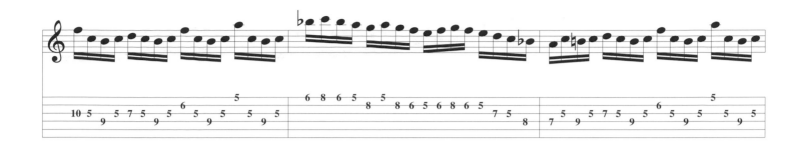

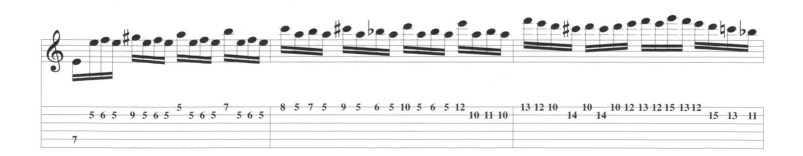

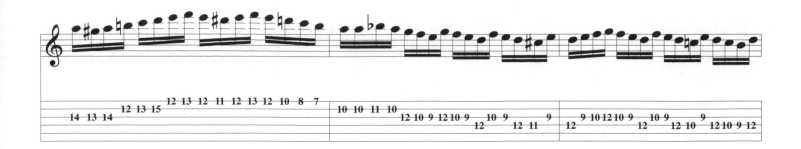

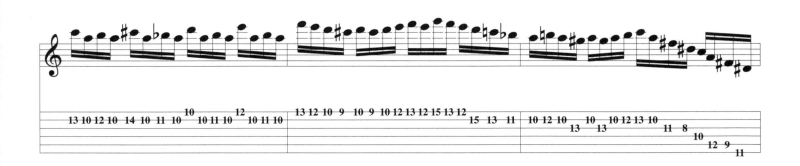

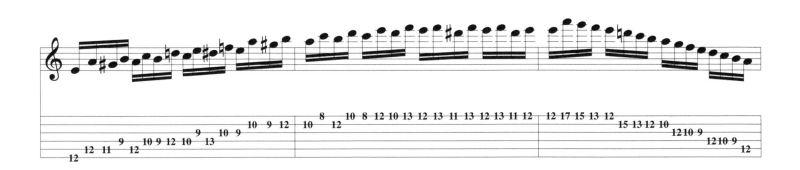

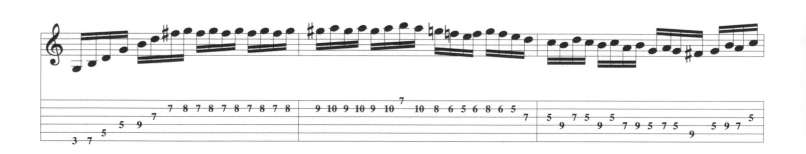

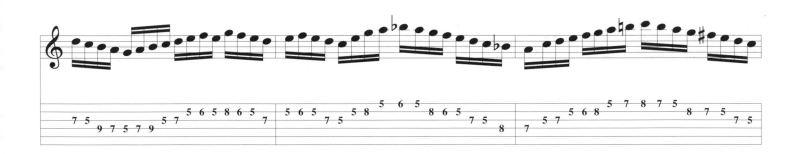

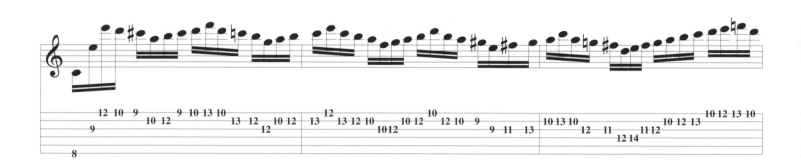

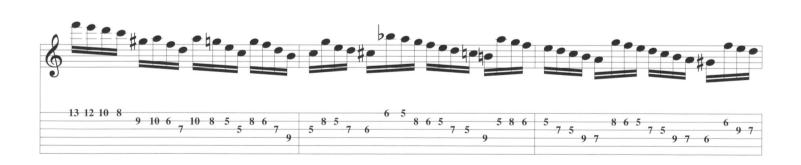

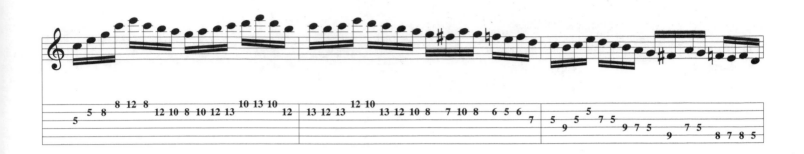

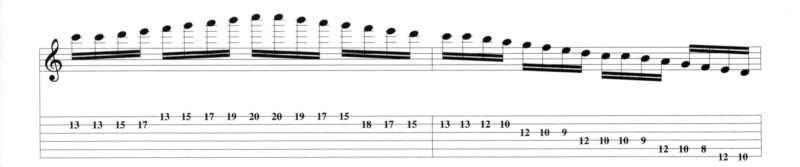

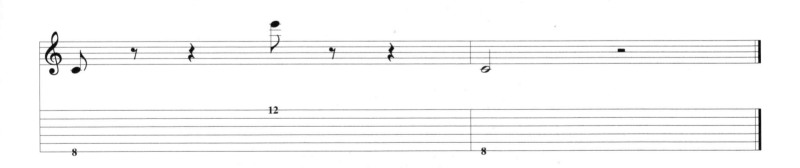

Wohlfahrt Study #3 Moderato

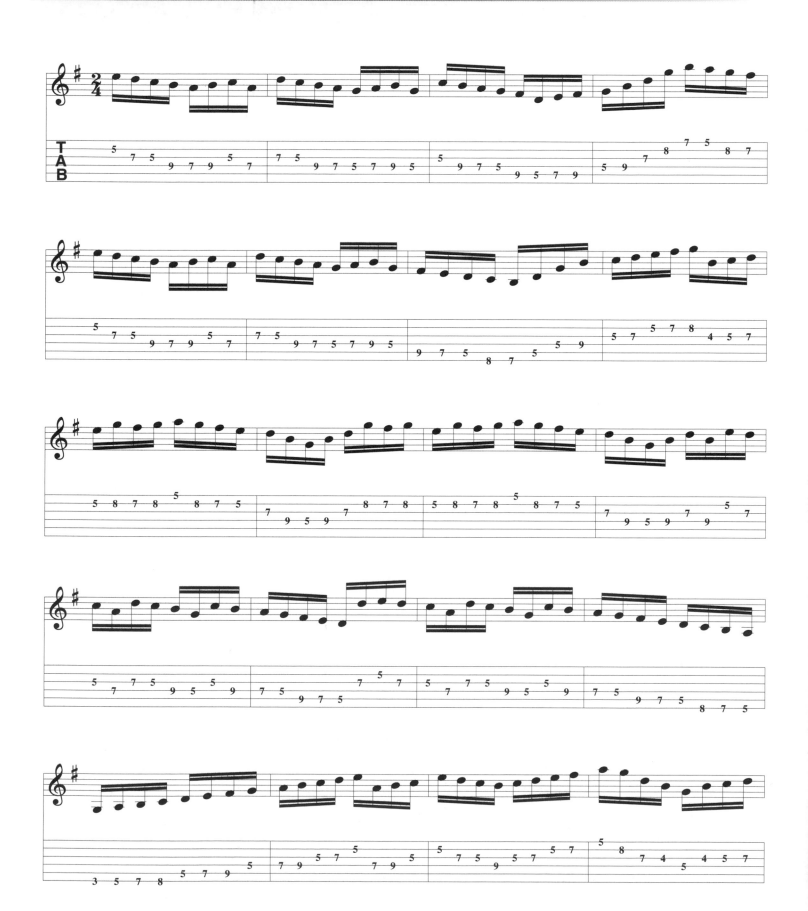

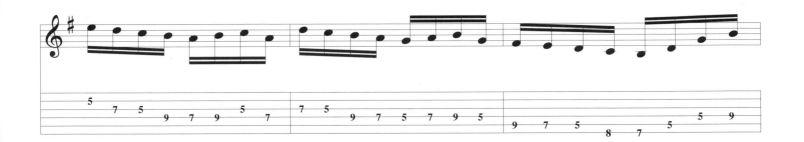

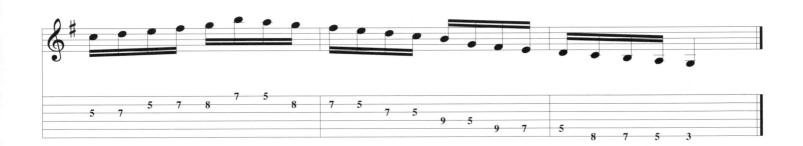